AAT

AF621707

Level 4

Diploma for Professional Accounting Technicians

Audit and Internal Controls

Course Book

From September 2026

BPP
LYCEUM EDUCATION GROUP

First edition 2026

ISBN 9781 0355 4446 2

ISBN (for internal use only) 9781 0355 4066 2

eISBN 9781 0355 4467 7

British Library Cataloguing-in-Publication Data

A catalogue record for this book is available from the British Library

Published by

BPP Learning Media Ltd
BPP House, Aldine Place
142–144 Uxbridge Road
London W12 8AA

learningmedia.bpp.com

Your learning materials are printed on paper obtained from traceable sustainable sources.

IFRS

Contents

Introduction to the course

Syllabus overview

This unit teaches students about the role and importance of internal controls within an organisation. Students will explore the purpose and components of internal controls and understand how they impact organisations. All organisations must guard against fraud through good internal control systems. A key aim of this unit is to provide students with the tools to identify fraud risks and assess how internal controls can be used to mitigate those risks.

Students will cover the concepts and principles of audit and assurance, gaining a clear understanding of the regulatory environment and the role of corporate governance. The unit distinguishes between internal and external audits and explains the broader context within which audits are conducted and the standards that guide these processes.

The unit will provide students with an awareness of the audit process from planning and risk assessment to the final completion and production of the audit report. Understanding the audit risk model and the concept of materiality will enable students to contribute effectively to the planning of audits.

Students will understand how internal controls influence audit approaches and learn to evaluate and test these controls effectively. This includes determining when to use a combination of tests of controls and substantive procedures, or substantive procedures alone, ensuring that audits are thorough and reliable.

Furthermore, the unit explores various audit assertions and procedures, sampling techniques, and methods for obtaining sufficient and appropriate audit evidence. Students will be able to identify suitable audit procedures and understand the reliability and relevance of different sources of audit evidence, including digital techniques.

Finally, the unit focuses on reviewing and reporting audit findings. Students will learn to assess audit findings, identify deficiencies in internal controls, and report these findings to management and audit committees.

Students will require an understanding of Financial Accounting, as this knowledge will be used during the practical application of audit techniques.

Test specification for this unit assessment

Assessment method	Marking type	Duration of assessment
Computer based assessment	Wholly computer marked	2 hours

Learning outcomes and objectives		Weighting
1	Understand the role of internal controls within an organization	30%
2	Understand the audit and assurance framework	15%
3	Understand the planning and risk assessment process for audit engagements	10%
4	Evaluate internal control systems as part of the audit process	10%
5	Understand procedures for obtaining sufficient and appropriate evidence	25%
6	Review and report findings	10%
Total		**100%**

Assessment structure

- Duration: 2 hours
- Competency is 70%
- The total number of marks for this assessment is 100

Note. This is only a guideline as to what might come up, based on the AAT's sample. The format and content of each task may vary from what we have listed below.

Your assessment will consist of nine tasks.

The assessment will take the form of a computer-based test. The assessment will require computer marking and the results will be available instantly.

Task	Learning outcomes and objectives	Max marks	Chapter ref	Study complete
1	1.1 Internal controls and their impact on organisations	10	Chapter 1	
2	1.2 Control objectives, risks and control procedures	10	Chapter 1	
3	1.3 Fraud	10	Chapter 1	
4	2.1-2.4 The audit and assurance framework	15	Chapter 2	
5	3.1-3.2 The planning and risk assessment process for audit engagements	10	Chapter 3	
6	4.1 Internal controls and their impact on the audit approach	10	Chapter 4	
7	5.1-5.3 Audit assertions, audit procedures and sampling	15	Chapters 4 and 5	
8	5.1 and 5.3 Audit evidence and the use of digital techniques in auditing	10	Chapters 4 and 5	
9	6.1-6.2 Audit findings	10	Chapter 6	

Skills bank

Our experience of preparing students for this type of assessment suggests that to obtain competency, you will need to develop a number of key skills.

1 Learning and applying the theory

2 Logical approaches to tasks

3 Effective use of your time in the assessment

What do I need to know to do well in the assessment?

It requires good overall awareness of many parts of your AAT studies so far and should be seen as an ideal way of applying much of what you have already learnt as context for the new content that you will see, showing how audits are conducted in practice.

To be successful in the assessment you need to:

- Know the new material introduced in each chapter, having practised a number of tasks that reflect the real assessment.
- Apply the techniques demonstrated to 'real life' situations as presented in each task. These will often be tested using scenarios where you can consider what would really happen if you were the auditor.

Assumed knowledge

Audit and Internal Controls is one of the Level 4 units. You need to understand the two Level 2 units, *Introduction to Bookkeeping* and *Principles of Bookkeeping Controls*, the Level 3 unit, *Financial Accounting: Preparing Financial Statements*, and *Financial Accounting*, covered at Level 4, before taking this unit.

Assessment style

In the assessment you could complete tasks by:

(a) Entering narrative by selecting from drop down menus of narrative options known as **picklists**

(b) Using **drag and drop** menus to enter narrative

(c) Typing in numbers, known as **gapfill** entry

(d) Entering **ticks**

You must familiarise yourself with the style of the online questions and the AAT software before taking the assessment. As part of your revision, log in to the **AAT website** and attempt its **online practice assessments**, found within the 'Lifelong Learning Portal'.

Introduction to the assessment

The question practice you do will prepare you for the format of tasks you will see in the *Audit and Internal Controls* assessment. It is also useful to familiarise yourself with the introductory information you **may** be given at the start of the assessment. For example:

- This assessment contains **nine tasks** and you should attempt to complete **every** task.
- Each task is independent. You will not need to refer to your answers to previous tasks.
- The total number of marks for this assessment is **100**.
- Read every task carefully to make sure you understand what is required.
- Where the date is relevant, it is given in the task data.

- Both minus signs and brackets can be used to indicate negative numbers **unless** task instructions state otherwise.
- You must use a full stop to indicate a decimal point. For example, write 100.57 **not** 100,57 or 10057.
- You may use a comma to indicate a number in the thousands, but you don't have to. For example, 10000 and 10,000 are both acceptable.
- You will need to double click to enter values into a gapfill or cell within a table.

Once you have clicked 'Continue' you will not be able to return to this page. You will be able to view the 'Assessment information' in the references section at each task position.

(a) As you revise, use the **BPP Passcards** to consolidate your knowledge. They are a revision tool perfect for packing in that last-minute revision.

(b) Attempt as many tasks as possible in the **Exam Practice kit**. There are plenty of assessment-style tasks which are excellent preparation for the real assessment.

(c) Always **check** through your own answers as you will in the real assessment, before looking at the solutions in the back of the Exam Practice Kit.

Key to icons

KEY TERM

Key term

A key definition which is important to be aware of for the assessment.

Formula to learn

A formula you will need to learn as it will not be provided in the assessment.

Formula provided

A formula which is provided within the assessment and generally available as a pop-up on screen.

Activity

An example which allows you to apply your knowledge to the technique covered in the Course Book. The solution is provided at the end of the chapter.

Illustration

A worked example which can be used to review and see how an assessment question could be answered.

Assessment focus point

A high priority point for the assessment.

Open book reference

Where use of an open book will be allowed for the assessment.

Real life examples

A practical real life scenario.

AAT qualifications

The material in this book may support the following AAT qualifications:

AAT Level 4 Diploma for Professional Accounting Technicians

Supplements

From time to time we may need to publish supplementary materials to one of our titles. This can be for a variety of reasons, from a small change in the AAT unit guidance to new legislation coming into effect between editions.

You should check our supplements page regularly for anything that may affect your learning materials. All supplements are available free of charge on our supplements page on our website at:

learningmedia.bpp.com/pages/resources-for-students

Improving material and removing errors

BPP Learning Media do everything possible to ensure the material is accurate and up to date when sending to print. In the event that any errors are found after the print date, they are uploaded to the following website:

learningmedia.bpp.com/pages/aat-errata

These learning materials are based on the qualification specification released by the AAT in November 2025.

AAT Practice Assessment

The AAT practice assessments mimic the real exam and so must be attempted prior to taking the real exam. You should attempt these using a laptop/desktop computer, as this will give you a better feel for the actual AAT exam conditions.

Please note, at the end of each test you will be presented with feedback which you should review.

Use this link below to access the assessment required:

https://www.aat.org.uk/learning-portal.

Glossary of terms

It is useful to be familiar with interchangeable terminology including IFRS and UK GAAP (generally accepted accounting principles).

Below is a short list of the most important terms you are likely to use or come across, together with their international and UK equivalents.

UK term	International term
Profit and loss account	Statement of profit or loss (or statement of profit or loss and other comprehensive income)
Turnover or Sales	Revenue or sales revenue
Operating profit	Profit from operations
Reducing balance depreciation	Diminishing balance depreciation
Depreciation/depreciation expense(s)	Depreciation charge(s)
Balance sheet	Statement of financial position
Fixed assets	Non-current assets
Net book value	Carrying amount
Tangible assets	Property, plant and equipment
Stocks	Inventories
Trade debtors or debtors	Trade receivables
Prepayments	Other receivables
Debtors and prepayments	Trade and other receivables
Cash at bank and in hand	Cash and cash equivalents
Long-term liabilities	Non-current liabilities

UK term	International term
Trade creditors or creditors	Trade payables
Accruals	Other payables
Creditors and accruals	Trade and other payables
Capital and reserves	Equity (limited companies)
Profit and loss balance	Retained earnings
Cash flow statement	Statement of cash flows

Accountants often have a tendency to use several phrases to describe the same thing! Some of these are listed below:

Different terms for the same thing
Nominal ledger, main ledger or general ledger
Subsidiary ledgers, memorandum ledgers
Subsidiary (sales) ledger, sales ledger
Subsidiary (purchase) ledger, purchase ledger

1 Internal controls and fraud

Learning outcomes

1	**Understand the role of internal controls within an organisation**
1.1	**Internal controls and their impact on the organisation** Students need to understand: 1.1.1 the purpose of internal controls: • facilitate operations • safeguard assets • prevent and detect fraud • ensure quality of internal and external reporting • compliance with laws and regulations 1.1.2 the components of internal control: • the control environment • the entity's risk assessment process • the entity's process to monitor the systems of internal control • the information system and communication • control activities 1.1.3 the types of internal controls used in different parts of the accounting function: • authorisation and approval • general IT controls • information processing controls • organisational • personnel • physical or logical controls • reconciliations • segregation of duties • supervision • verifications 1.1.4 the limitations of internal controls 1.1.5 how different types of internal controls suit different types of organisations: • size (small and medium, large) • nature (cash-based, credit-based, online).
1.2	**Control objectives, risks and procedures** Learners need to understand:

	1.2.1 control objectives for accounting systems: • sales • purchases • payroll • inventory • non-current assets • bank and cash 1.2.2 risks within accounting systems 1.2.3 control procedures for accounting systems.

1.3	**Managing fraud risk**
	Learners need to understand:
	1.3.1 the common types of fraud within a business:
	• fraudulent financial reporting
	• misappropriation of assets
	1.3.2 the fraud risk assessment process:
	• identify the risk
	• evaluate the risk
	• respond to the risk
	  - manage
	  - mitigate
	• ensure legal and regulatory compliance
	• monitor, review and report
	1.3.3 implications for an organisation if fraud occurs:
	• financial
	• non-financial
	Learners need to be able to:
	1.3.4 identify the circumstances when fraud may occur
	1.3.5 evaluate the impact of fraud on an organisation:
	• financial
	• non-financial
	1.3.6 assess how internal controls can be used in preventing and detecting fraud.

Assessment context

The topics covered in this chapter will be included within Tasks 1, 2 and 3 in the Audit and Internal Controls unit assessment.

Qualification context

While it is possible some of this content may be familiar, you should consider it all to be new to this Level.

Business context

The system of internal controls is designed to ensure the company does not fall prey to fraud, error or misstatement of its financial statements. This ensures that the company can operate effectively. The different types of controls within an organisation are identified and explanations as to why they would be important for an accounting system. These are then reviewed in terms of the sales, purchases (including non-current assets) and payroll systems, with activity practice.

Chapter overview

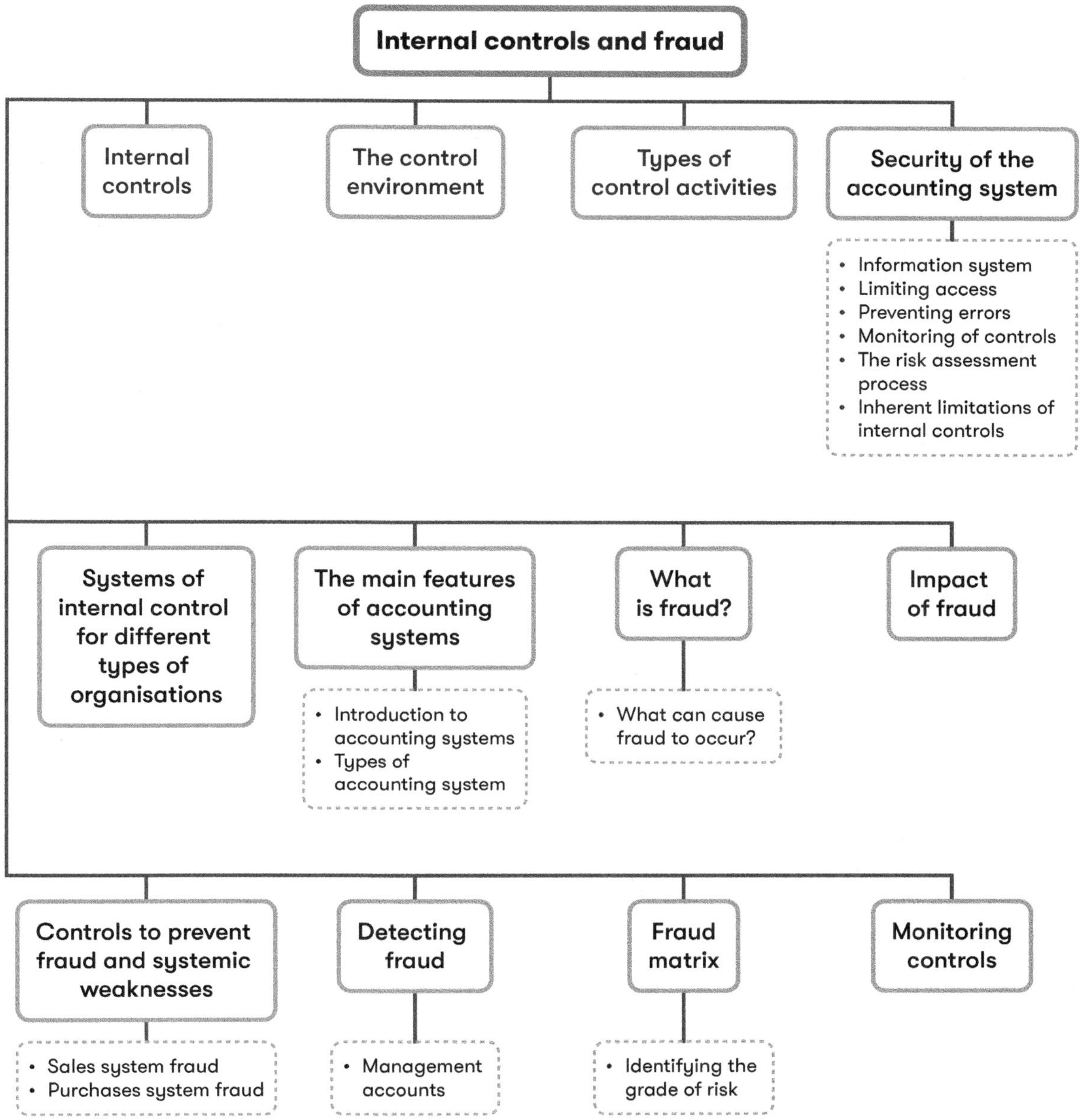

Introduction

In this chapter we look at the purpose and type of internal controls commonly found in an organisation.

A strong system of internal controls minimises financial loss within an organisation and can ensure that ethical standards are maintained.

Weak controls are one of the reasons that fraud may occur within an organisation. We will look at the common types of fraud and the implications of fraud within an organisation.

Organisations need to have good internal controls to prevent fraud taking place, with particular focus on the importance of the segregation of duties within the accounting function.

Accounting systems are at risk of specific frauds, namely payroll fraud, payables ledger fraud and receivables ledger fraud. We will look at the controls that should be in place to prevent these.

1 Internal controls

KEY TERM

> **Internal controls:** Policies and procedures that address the risk that the aims and objectives of the company will not be met.

The purpose of internal controls is to:

- Facilitate operations
- Safeguard assets
- Prevent and detect fraud
- Ensure quality of internal and external reporting
- Comply with laws and regulations

Internal controls work alongside the control environment to create the overall control framework. This is known as the **system of internal control**.

KEY TERM

> **System of internal control:** The control environment, the entity's risk assessment process, the entity's processes to monitor the system of internal control, the information system and communication and control activities.
>
> **Systemic weaknesses:** Weaknesses that arise within the accounting system itself, which leave it open to fraud and error.

Robust systems of internal control:

- Reduce systemic weaknesses in the accounting system, including the scope for errors
- Reduce the risk of loss or fraud
- Ensure that the accounting system operates appropriately
- Ensure the accounting system can change in line with the environment and organisational requirements
- Ensure that ethical standards are met within an organisation

In very broad terms, systems of internal control are designed to make sure that **good things** happen to an entity while **avoiding any bad things** at the same time. Not all entities have the same **approach** to setting up their internal controls, however, and this is frequently determined by the control environment – so what is the **control environment**?

2 The control environment

KEY TERM

> **Control environment:** Formed by the attitudes, awareness and actions of management and those responsible for ensuring that the internal controls within the company meet that company's needs.

The control environment is part of the system of internal controls, alongside the internal controls themselves.

The owners or management of a company must ensure that these control activities are **regularly monitored** to ensure that nothing goes wrong. If the controls are not followed and management do nothing in response, the system of internal controls will not operate effectively, eg if a manager knowingly authorises a fraudulent expense claim by a subordinate, then the internal control requiring expenses to be authorised by management is undermined by the weak control environment.

Management must regularly assess the **existing** system and **identify any new risks** which may affect how robust the control system currently is. Without this monitoring, there is unlikely to be a strong control environment.

Indications of a **good control environment** include the following:

(a) Management communicate and enforce integrity and ethical behaviour.

(b) Management and staff are well trained and competent.

(c) Management operates in a way that promotes control, eg regularly monitoring whether the controls are working and adhered to in practice.

(d) The company and accounting function is structured in a way that promotes control.

(e) Authority and responsibility for controls is assigned to separate people ie segregation of duties is commonplace.

(f) Human resources policies promote controls.

(g) Management regularly review and reassess any new or potential risks to assess whether the controls in place are robust enough to ensure a strong control environment.

3 Types of control activities

KEY TERM

Control activities: Policies and procedures that help ensure that objectives are carried out.

Segregation of duties: Making sure that more than one person is involved in different parts of each process to minimise the opportunity for fraud and error.

Physical controls: Ensuring assets such as inventory and cash are safe by means of locked rooms and containers, cameras and security staff.

The types of control activity that should be used in an accounting system to address systemic weaknesses can be remembered using the mnemonic **SPAMSOAP**:

(a) **S**egregation of duties – eg different members of staff should (1) open the post, (2) record any cash or cheques received and (3) bank cash or cheques received. These can be built into integrated computer systems, eg an invoice is raised by one user, but a manager must log in to approve them. Others may be manual, such as proof of authorisation by a signature on a hard copy report.

(b) **P**hysical controls – controls over the physical security of accounting records and assets such as cash and inventory, eg lock cash receipts in a safe until they are banked; require codes to unlock the cash tills; lock the stores where inventory is kept.

(c) **A**uthorisation controls

KEY TERM

Authorisation and approval of transactions: Undertaken by supervisors and managers – this shows the person processing the transaction that it is valid, eg overtime should be approved by departmental heads.

Authorisation controls: These ensure that only authorised personnel can make changes, such as to standing data or to authorise a bank payment.

(d) **M**anagement controls – managers should review whether control activities are being carried out within the accounting system, eg comparing budget to actual performance in a budgetary control report, and comparing performance and position from one period to the next using ratio analysis.

(e) **S**upervision controls – there should be close oversight of people performing accounting tasks day to day.

KEY TERM

> **Reviews:** Performed by supervisors or managers by looking at summaries and reports of transactions, eg to ensure they are reasonable.

(f) **O**rganisation – the way tasks and the business as a whole are organised should support internal control eg clear lines of responsibility, delegation and reporting, and adequate resources being available for the accounting system.

(g) **A**rithmetic and accounting controls – whether transactions have been processed accurately and completely eg **reconciliations** such as a bank statement and a cash book, or a payables ledger account and a statement from the supplier, can also highlight if errors have occurred

KEY TERM

> **Accounting controls:** Controls which help to identify mistakes in the accounting records.

Other accounting controls can be highlighted by a trial balance being out of balance or a computer system not allowing a journal to be posted where the debits do not equal the credits.

KEY TERM

> **Reconciliations:** Controls where staff ensure that two different sources of information agree or that any differences are understood, eg bank reconciliations verifying the bank statement to the bank account on the nominal ledger.
>
> **Verification:** The process of confirming that something is what it claims to be; in other words, that something can be said to be true. In accounting terms, this would include confirming an amount, date, name, location or event.

(h) **P**ersonnel controls – appropriately recruited, selected and trained accounting staff should be employed

Activity 1: The control environment

Consider the following scenario for a fictitious organisation called BCC Co that provides facilities services to a wide range of clients. A wide range of products is also sold by the company's retail outlet, which is located on the same site as the company's warehouse and main office.

> The accounts receivable clerk is the first to arrive at work on Monday morning. He opens the post and begins logging any cash and cheques received into the day book when the telephone rings. It is the senior accounts clerk, to say that she had an emergency dental appointment that morning, so she would be late for work. The accounts receivable clerk goes back to his task of processing the mail; without noticing, he has dropped a cheque behind the desk before he has written it into the day book. The accounts receivable clerk puts the day book, with the cheques inside, onto his desk while he goes to discuss the morning's deliveries with the warehouse manager.
>
> One of the directors is going out for lunch with a client later that day. As she is short on cash and does not have time to go to the bank, she helps herself to £40 from the petty cash tin, and tells the accounts receivable clerk that she will replace it this afternoon when she has returned from her lunch meeting.
>
> One of the supervisors has asked for assistance with some goods deliveries that need to be moved into the warehouse from the pallet delivery outside. Only one member of staff is certified to drive a forklift truck but he is on annual leave, so in his absence, one of the warehouse staff offers to move the goods as he has been shown how to use the forklift on a number of occasions. The supervisor accepts his offer.

The finance director is concerned that some customers are becoming increasingly slow in making payments on their credit accounts. He asks the accounts receivable clerk to prepare a schedule of receivables, but the clerk is busy drawing up the sales invoices (he uses a Word template and manually inputs details from the sales team) and asks if this could be done next month. The accounts receivable clerk has not chased up late payments recently because he is too busy. Constructing a receivables ledger from the Word document invoices takes at least two to three hours, and there is still a lot of post to be processed that morning.

The wages clerk, who has been on holiday, is approached by one of the sales team. He had been expecting commission totalling £800 in his wages, but the senior accounts clerk (who had covered for the wages clerk last month) had not processed this and had only prepared his wages based on his basic hours worked. He tells the wages clerk that he really needs this money but, knowing she could do nothing until the next wages run, the wages clerk tells him he would have to wait seven days.

The sales team member is so upset by this news that the wages clerk is consumed with guilt, and she tells him that she will borrow the money out of the petty cash tin and replace it when she makes his wages up next week.

The senior accounts clerk keeps the company cheque book in her drawer, but as she only works part time, the drawer is often left unlocked.

Required

Identify areas of weakness from the scenario above.

4 Security of the accounting system

The accounting system must be secure so that it can perform its function. This can be done in a number of ways, for instance preventing initial access to the system with a physical control (locks on the doors) or using passwords to prevent unauthorised access to the software.

KEY TERM

Information processing controls: Controls relating to the transactions and standing data in the computerised accounting system.

Integrity controls: Controls that verify and validate input data, the processing of data and the production of reports.

Logical controls: Controls related to preventing unauthorised access to data within a system.

4.1 Information system

Information systems support both **internal** and **external communications**. Within **information processing controls**, there are a number of specific controls that relate to **information technology** (IT) systems, although it must be remembered that an information system could just as easily be:

- A filing cabinet
- An integrated IT system

Information systems relevant to **financial reporting** should address the following:

- Identifying and recording all valid transactions
- Accurately reflect all transactions, including their timing, value and rationale for financial reporting purposes

IT controls tend to be separated into two categories: **general** and **application**.

General IT controls	Application IT controls
Policies and **procedures** relating to many applications, **supporting** the **effective functioning** of application controls: • Data centre and **networks** • Systems software change, acquisition and maintenance • Program change • Access **security** • Application system acquisition, development and maintenance	Manual or automated procedures that apply to the **processing** of transactions. They can be both **preventative** and **detective** in nature: • Initiating, recording, processing and reporting **transactions** • Authorisation, completeness, and accuracy at all stages (eg input data, numerical sequence checks, **exception reports** and correction at point of data entry)

Activity 2: Logical controls

Within information systems, there are integrity controls and both general and application IT controls. Logical controls are also relevant here when discussing access.

Required

Suggest some examples of logical controls.

4.2 Limiting access

KEY TERM

Security controls: Controls in the accounting system that cover integrity controls, system controls and physical access controls.

Management should guard against malicious or fraudulent access using a variety of **security controls**, such as physical barriers (locks on doors and cabinets), deterrents (alarm system or security), IT and other cyber security controls (ensuring adequate disaster recovery processes are in place, such as backups of data) and monitoring of controls (management reviews, authorisation requirements etc).

Such controls in the accounting system include implementing **integrity controls**.

There should be **information processing controls** over standing data to ensure only authorised changes are made; for example, new suppliers can only be entered onto a system by an authorised person, or payroll data only accessible by payroll staff.

Ensuring strict segregation of duties by reducing the number of people involved in different parts of each process and minimising the opportunity for fraud and error will help to ensure the integrity of standing data and ensuring only authorised transactions are made.

KEY TERM

Integrity of data: Ensures that data is complete, secure and accurate.

4.3 Preventing errors

The accounting system should have robust integrity controls to verify and validate input data, the processing of data and the production of reports.

These should include input controls on completeness of data input to the system (eg batch processing, total checks, not allowing journals to be posted which do not balance). There can also be programme controls ensuring the accuracy of data input to the system, such as an automatic check on the calculation of VAT. Some controls, such as integrity controls, check the consistency and validity of the data being entered eg the correct format of figures are used (eg allowing invoice numbers in the correct format, AA12345) and reviewing the calculation of VAT. They are rules in the system which allow only certain types of data to be inserted.

KEY TERM

Processing controls: May be used to warn the user if they try to log out before processing is finished or close a document prior to saving. Data is also reviewed for arithmetical accuracy.

Processing controls verify the data validation and editing procedures. They can also ensure that forms are not closed without being saved or can only be altered by one user at a time. They also used for ensuring arithmetical accuracy or completeness of data. One example of this is 'batch invoice processing' whereby the total value of the invoices is independently calculated and then the total of the invoices entered onto the system is verified against this total.

4.4 Monitoring of controls

A further component of a good system of internal control is **monitoring** – those activities that the entity uses to **keep an eye on** how well it is **achieving its objectives** and how the entity initiates **remedial action** to **address deficiencies** in control. Examples of monitoring include:

- **Management** controls such as reviewing whether a bank reconciliation is prepared on a timely basis and following up on any areas of non-compliance. Such controls can be either **preventative controls**) (designed to reduce the occurrence of errors and deviations – eg secure storage of inventory in a warehouse) or **detective controls** (designed to identify errors and deviations once they have occurred – eg a burglar alarm). Monitoring the effectiveness of each will help an entity decide whether it requires more of one or the other when establishing controls.
- **Internal audit** (a specific department within an entity that monitors all aspects of the entity and reports its findings to those charged with governance)
- Other governance arrangements (such as the use of an audit committee staffed with non-executive directors representing the interests of shareholders)
- **Information systems** designed not only to report but also to interrogate data
- **Communication channels** with **stakeholders** (eg customer feedback or liaison with regulators

4.5 The risk assessment process

We have already discussed how management should regularly review the controls that are in place. In doing so, any review should assess the ability of the system of internal control to respond to the risk that:

(a) **Objectives might not be met** – including the company's sustainability and corporate social reporting (CSR) objectives (eg sales targets, waste disposal, staff training requirements and recruitment concerns)

(b) The company may be the victim of **loss or fraud** – can be accidental or intended, and arise from internal or external sources

(c) The system may contain errors that result in **misstatement in the financial statements** – eg assets overvalued and/or liabilities understated

(d) The company is engaged in **unethical behaviour** – either intentionally (eg due to pressures to achieve unrealistic sales targets) or unintentionally (eg poorly trained staff taking on new tasks)

(e) The company **fails to comply with its legal obligations** – such as non-compliance with company law or health and safety regulations

The **risk assessment process** is used to determine which controls are necessary. Fraud risk assessments should be carried out on a **continuous basis** because fraud risk is always present. The risk assessment process consists of the following stages:

Step 1 **Identify the risk** – this includes activities such as gathering information about processes within an organisation, listing potentially fraudulent schemes and understanding the organisational structure.

This should include an assessment of any new risks, both **internal** (such as a new computer system or management restructure) and **external** (increased market competition, issues with suppliers etc) that may impact the organisation.

Step 2 **Evaluate the risk** – this takes into consideration the **likelihood** of the fraud occurring and the **impact** if it does occur.

Step 3 **Respond to the risk** – organisations may have a variety of different responses depending on the risks that have been evaluated:

- If likelihood and impact are considered low, the risk may just be accepted and either ignored or monitored for any change
- For low impact risks that are more likely, the risk would need to be managed by an effective control

- Some risks may be evaluated as very unlikely to occur, but if they did occur, their impact would be great – in such cases, transferring the risk to a third party (for example, via an insurance policy) may be preferable.
- Finally, for high-risk items in terms of both likelihood and impact, alternative courses of action may be required (such as avoiding the activity that leads to the risk or similar).

Step 4 **Ensure legal and regulatory compliance** – any response should comply with all relevant laws, regulations and best practice.

Step 5 **Monitor, review and report** – this is covered in more detail towards the end of this chapter, but in essence, this is an ongoing process designed to ensure that fraud risks are not ignored.

Activity 3: Payroll risks

Read the following information about the payroll operated by BCC Co.

> The warehouse manager is explaining to the wages clerk that he had to take on an extra member of staff for the busy season. He says that the new employee would be paid on an hourly basis, and that as he was a student, he would not pay any tax and could be paid weekly in cash. The wages clerk asks for the new starter documentation that all new employees have to complete, but the warehouse manager shouts her down, insisting that this is not necessary for temporary staff and that she should just add him to the payroll system. He says that he will send through the completed documentation later in the week. The wages clerk reluctantly agrees and adds the new worker to the payroll, leaving herself a diary note to ask the warehouse manager for the documentation next week if it is still outstanding. The warehouse manager takes £1,200 from petty cash to cover the new employee's wages and tells the wages clerk to replace it when she makes up the next week's payroll.
>
> Later that day, the printer used by the wages clerk jams, resulting in several payslips being printed upside down. The wages clerk screws up the partially torn and smudged payslips into a ball and throws them in the bin. She then assures the directors that she will re-run the payslips first thing the next day, and goes home early.

Required

Identify the risks present in the payroll system described above. Highlight the key issues which have occurred in the payroll system and what regulatory and ethical risks these pose to the organisation.

4.6 Inherent limitations of internal controls

However good any single element of a system of internal control might be, no system can ever be perfect, due to inherent limitations.

Internal controls are usually designed to operate **as effectively as the entity considers appropriate** in the context of its **control environment**. However, the internal controls in place within an entity can only ever provide **reasonable assurance** that they will achieve the entity's

objectives. In other words, there are always going to be **some inherent limitations of internal controls**.

The inherent limitations of the effectiveness of internal controls include:

- People make mistakes that may not be picked up by software or human review (**human error**).
- People **may not operate controls properly**, thus making them redundant.
- People may **deliberately** circumvent control systems if they want to defraud the company, either individually, or by colluding together.
- Lack of review of the controls in place means that there is **no incentive for staff to follow them.**
- An **overreliance on controls**, especially computerised controls, can breed complacency meaning errors go undetected.

Activity 4: Inherent limitations of internal controls

For each of the following examples, identify the inherent limitation in the system of internal control.

Example	Human error ✓	Cost/benefit ✓	Fraud ✓	Non-routine ✓
Judgement can sometimes be faulty due to overconfidence, fatigue or stress				
No matter how well designed or implemented an internal control is, there is a risk of the control not being able to cope with a random item				
Two or more parties work together to bypass the segregation of duties				
A fund is set up to cover potential losses due to excessive insurance premiums				
The results of an exception report are misinterpreted				

5 Systems of internal control for different types of organisations

As regulation and reporting requirements become more complex, the underlying system of internal control must also be reviewed and assessed for suitability by management.

The level of complexity and size of the system of internal control will depend on the size and nature of the organisation.

Large companies produce significant amounts of data which is usually recorded electronically. Therefore, large companies usually need a mixture of controls over electronic data as well as some manual internal controls. Large companies usually have lots of staff which makes segregation of duties easier.

A **small or medium-sized company** may have fewer staff members to perform controls and therefore they are less able to implement segregation of duty. These companies might use simpler accounting systems with more manual controls.

Some businesses are **cash-based** but have good physical controls over cash and regular reconciliations to ensure that the cash balances are correct, for example reconciling the cash register balance at the end of the day: such businesses are usually considered to be riskier than a business that operates on credit.

Credit-based businesses tend to have a lot more documentation at each stage of their transaction cycles. This paper (or electronic) documentation makes it easier to establish an audit trail to implement internal controls and monitor whether they have been adhered to.

Online businesses will need different controls to physical businesses. As well as strong controls over their IT systems, there will need to be good physical controls over any inventory, especially as these businesses often have higher levels of returns.

6 The main features of accounting systems

6.1 Introduction to accounting systems

You know from your AAT studies already that an entity manages its own financial stability by having a collection of **systems** in place. Specific examples of such systems will follow but, for all of them, it is necessary to be able to understand control objectives, risks and control procedures:

KEY TERM

Control objectives: What a system is trying to do.

Risks: What a system is trying to avoid.

Control procedures: How a system achieves objectives and manages risks.

Activity 5: Control objectives, risks and control procedures – introduction

For each of the following activities found within a payroll system, select whether it is a control objective, a risk, or a control procedure, using the options listed below.

Activity	Type
Financial statements contain inaccurate payroll information	▼
Compare payroll costs with budget	▼
Confirm a sample of payslips to timesheets and staff contracts	▼
All pay and deductions should be accurately recorded	▼
Employees are paid for hours they have not worked	▼
Employees should only be paid for hours they have worked	▼

Picklist

- Control objective
- Control procedure
- Risk

6.2 Types of accounting system

These are the major accounting systems that you will need to know about:

- Purchases
- Revenue
- Payroll
- Inventory
- Non-current assets
- Cash and bank

The following activity will assist you in understanding what each of the major accounting systems looks like and how each one relies on an understanding of **control objectives**, **risks** and **control procedures**.

Activity 6: Control objectives, risks and procedures for systems

For each of the main accounting systems, can you think of some examples of control objectives, risks and control procedures?

Note. **This activity is designed to get you thinking about systems – the solutions are very thorough and presented for you to refer to as you study this unit.**

	Control objectives	Risks	Control procedures
Purchases			
Revenue			
Payroll			
Inventory			
Non-current assets			
Cash and bank			

7 What is fraud?

You were introduced to the concept of fraud and the regulations surrounding it during your Level 3 studies. It is useful to review the key points before attempting the activities in this section.

KEY TERM

> **Fraud:** A deliberate or intentional attempt to gain advantage by some form of deception.

Legally, there are three types of fraud (Fraud Act 2006: s.1):

- False representation
- Failure to disclose information
- Abuse of position

With respect to the accounting system, the types of fraud which are important are:

KEY TERM

> **Misappropriation of assets:** Theft, teeming and lading, payment of false employees or suppliers.
>
> **Misstatement of the financial statements:** The overstatement of assets or profit, or the understatement of profit, losses or liabilities.

An accounting system is more open to fraud if it contains systemic weaknesses, making it easy to misappropriate assets, or misstate financial information.

Examples of fraud include, but are not restricted to:

- Falsifying financial statements or documents, such as invoices
- Incorrect accounting to purposely hide debts or overstate profits
- False claims about the products being sold by the company (for example, Silicon Valley start-up Theranos)
- Payment fraud, including teeming and lading (misallocation of cash payments)
- Tax evasion, such as understatement of VAT, PAYE or corporate tax.
- Money laundering
- Insider trading
- Embezzlement (fraud by employees in positions of power or trust within a business), such as by creating fictitious suppliers or employees

7.1 What can cause fraud to occur?

Cressey (1973) explained that fraud was likely to occur if three conditions were present:

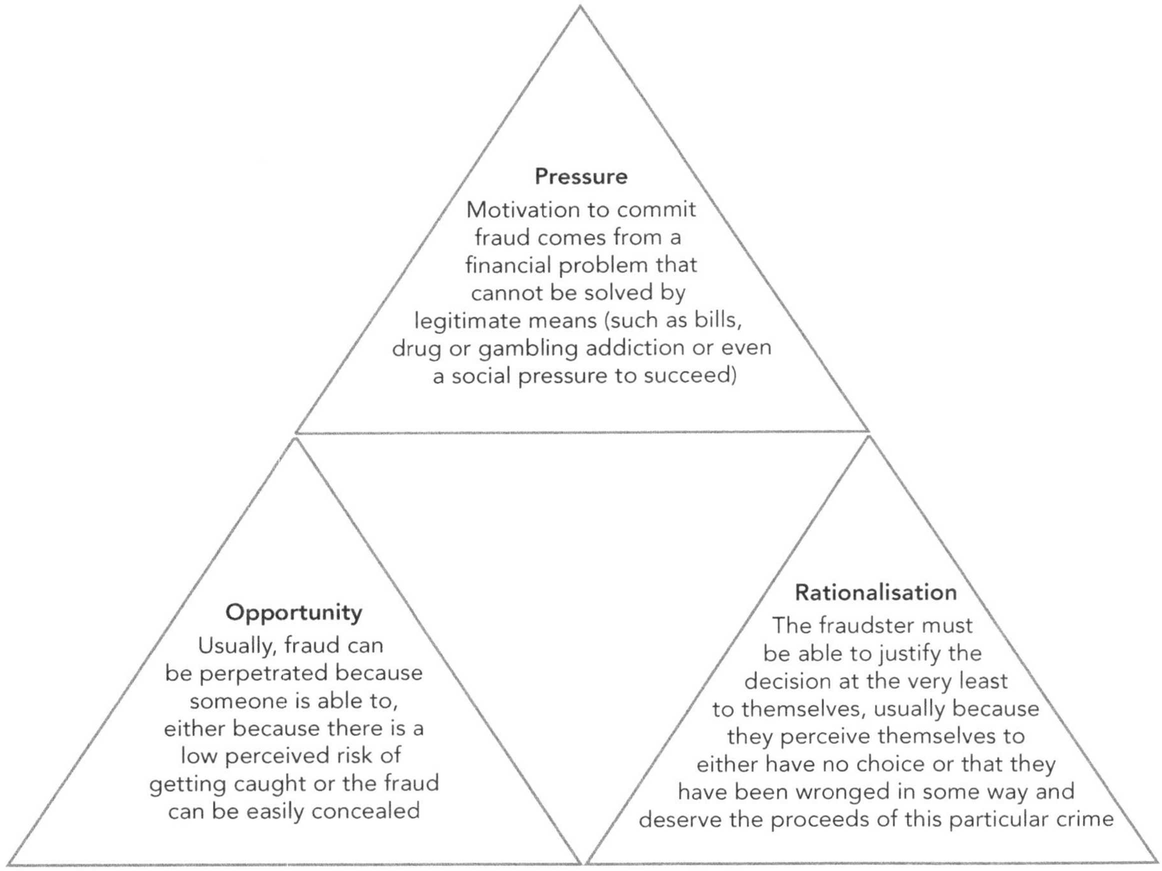

Knowing that fraud is usually a product of these three conditions means that an organisation can focus on each one when considering both **prevention** and **detection** of fraud. For example:

- **Pressure** – are staff likely to be affected by external factors, such as blackmail, addiction or extortion?
- **Opportunity** – are assets likely to be vulnerable (and are any of our internal controls poor)?
- **Rationalisation** – are staff disenfranchised or desperate enough to commit fraud, and do our recruitment procedures always check employee references for any previous fraudulent behaviour?

Having a better understanding of the conditions that need to be present for fraud to occur can help an organisation design **suitable controls** that can attempt to **address** such conditions. The fraud triangle is a good way of understanding these conditions.

8 Impact of fraud

Fraud has the following types of impact on a company:

(a) **Financial** – loss of funds or other assets. This in turn affects the company's profitability and the owner's investment in it. It can also affect the company's share price.

(b) **Reputation** – exposure to fraud can affect the company's reputation in the eyes of internal and external stakeholders. This in turn could lead to a loss of business.

(c) **Employee morale** – the trust of existing employees could be damaged. Future recruitment and retention of staff might also be affected.

The following examples illustrate the financial and reputational impacts upon companies which have been fined for financial misstatement, or not having sufficient fraud prevention controls in place.

Real life example: Tesco Stores

In March 2017, Tesco Stores was fined £129 million by the Serious Fraud Office (SFO) and ordered to set up an £85 million compensatory scheme for shareholders and bondholders who bought shares between the results announcement and the accounting misstatement being made public. Tesco settled out of court regarding charges of false accounting and misstatement of profits.

The impact on the company was a £214 million cash outflow, not including legal costs, with Tesco recording an exceptional charge of £235 million for the 2016/2017 accounting year end.

(Reuters, 2017)

Real life example: Rolls-Royce PLC

Rolls-Royce PLC was fined £497.5 million by the SFO in January 2017 in respect of 12 counts of conspiracy to corrupt, false accounting and failure to prevent bribery over a period of 30 years. In addition, the company was fined $170 million by to the US Department of Justice and $25 million by the Brazilian authorities.

(Rolls Royce plc, 2025)

Real life example: NatWest Bank

The Financial Conduct Authority (FCA) fined the National Westminster (NatWest) Bank £264.8 million for three offences of failing to comply with money laundering regulations regarding the activity of a commercial customer between November 2012 and June 2016. When originally taken on by the bank, Fowler Oldfield, a Bradford-based jewellery business, was not expected to deal in cash, but deposited around £365 million, including £264 million in cash, over the period in question. This activity was later confirmed to involve large-scale money laundering. The fine was levied because although the bank identified several red flags (including significant amounts of Scottish bank notes that would not have been typical for an English business, plus other concerns that were raised when cash was deposited at NatWest branches) no action was taken, allowing the money laundering to continue.

(FCA, 2021)

---

9 Controls to prevent fraud and systemic weaknesses

In this section, we look specifically at the types of fraud which can occur within the business, identify potential issues and consider their impact.

The management of a company have a duty to put in place adequate controls to safeguard the company and its assets. You have seen many of the safeguarding controls in your Level 4 studies and have also covered them earlier in this chapter (SPAMSOAP).

The main types of controls which can help prevent fraud include controls for the accounting system can be grouped into the following categories:

- **Staff controls** – segregation of duties
- **Management controls** – review of controls and regular checks on control activities
- **Physical controls** – locking away confidential files and ensuring office security
- **Information processing and general IT controls** – password protection, access limitations and integration of systems

KEY TERM

Fraud controls: Internal controls specifically against fraud in the areas of staff controls, management controls, physical controls and IT controls.

9.1 Sales system fraud

Fraud within the sales system is possible because the system involves the receipt of money, and this risk is more severe where this is in the form of cash, such as a shop.

Activity 7: Sales system fraud

The following is some further information about BCC Co. Assume the date is 10 January 20X3.

The accounts receivable clerk is tidying up in the office one evening and is surprised to discover two cheques behind a desk. One was dated 8 August 20X2, and the other 23 November 20X2. He puts them in the in-tray intending to bank them the next day.

One of the directors has asked for a copy of the aged receivables report, as he hasn't seen one for nearly four months. He is annoyed when he discovers that one of the credit accounts, opened for B. Braithwaite, has made no payments against credit given at all so far. This customer has received £1,000 worth of goods and services and paid an initial deposit in July 20X2 but has made no payment since then. The director asks the accounts receivable clerk to track back through the account, which shows that no credit reference agency was used to vet the customer before accepting their initial order. The accounts receivable clerk decides to contact the agency to check on this customer, only to find that he has a very poor credit score.

Meanwhile, the director continues to review the aged receivables report and discovers that not only have debts been written off without his knowledge but also that over 50% of the invoices over 60 days old have no payments allocated against them. Unallocated cash amounts to £5,645.

The accounts receivable clerk reports that a large debt of £2,300 was written off the previous month, as it dated back to the previous October. He says that although he tried to chase the debt, the telephone number rang out. No delivery address has been logged by the sales staff.

When the director comes to lock up the retail outlet at the end of the day, he discovers that the tills have not been emptied or reconciled to the day's takings.

Required

(a) **Identify the types of fraud which could occur in the sales system at BCC Co based on the information you have been given in this extract. You should also explain why you think this fraud risk has arisen.**

You should structure your answer in the form of a table, with each fraud risk listed in the left-hand column and why the fraud risk has arisen in the right-hand column.

(b) **Consider the financial and non-financial impacts these frauds could have on BCC Co.**

9.2 Purchases system fraud

Fraud within the purchases system is possible because the system includes the ability to order goods from suppliers and then to make payments.

One of the general controls in place to prevent such examples of fraud is segregation of duties: the same member of the accounting team should not be allowed to place orders with suppliers, book in goods received, and then process payments to them.

Activity 8: Purchases system fraud

The following events happened at BCC Co during March 20X3:

> The senior accounts clerk needs to place a stationery order. She asks the company's staff what they need and places the order, including some additional paper for her nephew who is studying at university.
>
> PP Co, one of BCC Co's major suppliers, has requested urgent payment of an invoice that has been outstanding for 60 days. This invoice is for £15,000 and, though this would normally have been paid, there were not enough funds in the bank to cover this amount.
>
> When the senior accounts clerk informs the director of this, he is very surprised at the size of the invoice and asks her to review all the Goods Received Notes (GRNs) from PP Co to see what would have led to such a large invoice. The senior accounts clerk spends a day completing this reconciliation and discovers an error: the company has been charged for 1,000 boxes of consumables instead of 100, this having a wholesale price of £15.00 per box including VAT.
>
> When the director is checking the invoice, he asks the senior accounts clerk to produce a report of outstanding invoices and discovers some new suppliers with long outstanding debts which he does not recognise.

Required

Identify the risks from the control weaknesses in the above extract and make any recommendations to improve the controls.

Ensure your answer is specific to the scenario.

---

10 Detecting fraud

Internal controls within the accounting system should be designed not only to address weaknesses and prevent fraud and errors, but also to help detect when they have occurred.

The key controls that detect whether fraud or errors have occurred are:

(a) **Spot checks** on whether control activities have taken place

(b) **Performance reviews** and comparisons, using:

 (i) The **budgetary control report**: compare actual results to budgeted results

 (ii) **Ratio analysis**: compare this period to the previous period, and evaluate the relationships between figures in the financial statements (eg level of receivables compared with level of sales)

(c) **Reconciliation** of information produced by the accounting system with external evidence, such as bank statements and supplier statements

(d) **Control accountreconciliations** where transactions are recorded in individual accounts and in total (eg receivables and payables)

Management can use financial information to analyse and review the controls of an organisation. Financial information can highlight issues such as potential inefficiencies as well as possible fraudulent behaviour, eg decreases in profit margin may suggest that costs are being poorly managed, or may highlight an issue such as theft of inventory.

10.1 Management accounts

Management reports can be structured to ensure that the most useful information is available to the user of the report. The information may be summarised into a form of profit or loss statement, or include additional information such as variance analysis, aged receivables analysis or capital expenditure review for the period.

Ideally, these reports should be consistently prepared and monitored on a regular basis, eg monthly, so as to highlight any significant issues arising, and to prompt investigations and corrective action where required.

Activity 9: Detecting fraud using financial information

The following are some extracts from the management accounts which were completed at the year-end for BCC Co. The company completes quarterly management accounts only.

Extracts from the management accounts for BCC Co as at 31 December 20X2

	20X2		20X1	
	Products	Services	Products	Services
	£000	£000	£000	£000
Revenue	379	727	425	505
Cost of sales	(287)	(416)	(282)	(351)
Gross margin	**92**	**311**	**143**	**154**

	All activity		All activity	
	£000	£000	£000	£000
Rent and rates	30		30	
Salaries: administration and management	87		87	
Salaries: sales	105		60	
Salaries: directors	120		110	
Motor expenses	19		10	
Irrecoverable debts	22		8	
Finance costs	5		6	
Other costs	13		10	
Total costs		**401**		**321**
Net profit/(loss)		**2**		**(24)**

Required

Using the knowledge you have obtained from the earlier activities, review the management accounts above and highlight areas which present potential issues for the company, making any recommendations you believe are appropriate.

Note. **There is no requirement to calculate ratios.**

11 Fraud matrix

KEY TERM

> **Fraud matrix:** A map of the potential frauds against an organisation, cross-referenced to the risks of each of these occurring, documenting the controls over these risks. Also known as a risk matrix.

A fraud matrix helps the company:

- Investigate the **potential** for fraud within a system
- Analyse the **controls** currently in place to prevent fraud
- **Grade the potential** for fraud, according to risk

Although this approach is subjective, it enables a risk-based approach to improving controls that are appropriate to the company.

The risk to the company is graded on an appropriate scale, either numerically on a scale of 1–5 or by stating the deemed level of risk.

- 1 = low
- 3 = medium
- 5 = high

Possible improvements to the controls for all high and/or medium risks can then be recommended.

11.1 Identifying the grade of risk

The level of risk of fraud in a particular situation is graded as high, medium or low by identifying two factors:

- The **likelihood** of the risk occurring; and
- The potential **impact** of that risk on the company.

Illustration 1: BCC Co

In looking at the potential for the misappropriation of petty cash in BCC Co:

- The likelihood is high (5): loose cash is easy to steal and it presents a strong temptation, especially in small amounts, as the person stealing it may not perceive the loss to be that 'bad' a thing for the company.
- The impact on the company is medium (3), as the company could potentially lose £800.

Combining these two factors, the overall risk of fraud in relation to petty cash would probably be graded as medium/high (4).

12 Monitoring controls

Controls must be monitored to assess their effectiveness over time.

This review is usually overseen by management or, in larger organisations, an independent internal audit team. Internal auditors will review controls across different departments within the company. The role of internal audit differs from that of the external audit. You will learn more about audits later in this course.

In smaller organisations, effective monitoring can take place, formally or informally, by function heads. For example, the sales director is likely to become aware of control deficiencies in the sales cycle, as they are responsible for managing the sales department's ongoing performance, so will investigate any reasons behind poor performance.

Assessment focus point

For the ATIC assessment, you may be required to select appropriate **monitoring**, **review** and **report** actions in response to an identified risk. It is important that you can define these terms in order to be able to apply them to a scenario.

KEY TERM

Monitoring, review and report: In this context, **monitoring** means looking at activity or behaviour related to a specified fraud risk because you need to know the extent of this activity or behaviour.

Review means gathering evidence of this activity or behaviour to understand the extent of this fraud risk.

Report means what you communicate to those higher up in the organisation as part of the overall risk management process.

Illustration 2: Monitoring, review and report at BCC Co

The fraud matrix that was completed for BCC Co included a number of fraud risks. For example:

- Overstatement of wages - additional cash being paid to staff for work not done
- Theft of inventory from the warehouse
- Writing off customer debts without authorisation

Required

How would you monitor, review and report on these fraud risks?

Solution

Fraud risk	Monitoring (activity/behaviour)	Review (evidence to collect)	Report (what gets communicated)
Overstatement of wages - additional cash being paid to staff for work not done	Budget overspend or adverse variance Payments outside of contracted terms	Comparison of contract rates with actual payments Reconciliation of wage rates to employees' contracts of employment	Amount of any wage overspend by cause (not due to overtime or prior period error)
Theft of inventory from the warehouse	Inventory recorded as received but unable to be found when required	Instances of inventory leaving the warehouse without a legitimate reason (eg valid sales order)	Amount of inventory moved without legitimate documentation
Writing off customer debts without authorisation	Sales that are cancelled by staff without the appropriate authority	Sales written off without appropriate supporting documentation (eg credit note or journal approved by a senior member of staff)	Percentage of sales written off without appropriate supporting documentation

Chapter summary

- Internal controls in the accounting system aim: to protect it from systemic weaknesses; avoid fraudulent activities and human error; ensure compliance with applicable laws and regulations; and ensure the company is working to meet its objectives.
- The system of internal controls consists of an effective control environment; the entity's risk assessment process; the entity's process to monitor the system of internal control; the information system and communication; and control activities.
- Control activities in an accounting system address systemic weaknesses and control risks.
- Control activities consist of segregation of duties; physical controls; authorisation and approval of transactions; management controls; supervision controls; organisational controls; arithmetic and accounting controls; and personnel controls. The SPAMSOAP mnemonic may help you remember these.
- Information processing controls affect transactions and consist of input controls, accuracy controls, authorisation checks, processing controls and controls over standing data.
- General IT controls protect the general computer environment.
- The limitations of controls include people making mistakes, where controls may not be operated effectively or where people may deliberately circumvent controls.
- For each control objective within a system, the risks controlled and control procedures need to be identified.
- Within any of the systems, segregation of duties – as far as it is possible given the size of the accounting function and the number of its staff – is a vital control.
- In the credit sales system, control objectives etc are identified for: taking orders and extending credit; dispatching and invoicing goods; recording and accounting for sales and returns; and receiving payment.
- In the purchases system, control objectives etc are identified for: ordering; receipt of goods and services; accounting; and payments.
- In the payroll system, control objectives etc are identified for: setting wages and salaries; recording; payments; and deductions.
- Fraud is a deliberate or intentional attempt to gain advantage by some form of deception and for accounting systems includes either the misappropriation of assets or fraudulent financial reporting.
- A fraud matrix uses the impact and likelihood of fraud to map possible frauds within an organisation.

Activity answers

Activity 1: The control environment

Within this organisation, controls are very informal. Reliance is often based on trust. Formal internal controls would support the accounting system and reduce the possibility of fraud occurring.

Petty cash – no control system is in place. People can help themselves to cash as and when needed; there is no control or reconciliation at the end of each day. The director feels she is able to help herself to petty cash.

Cash and cheques received in the post are not secured away in a locked drawer or a safe prior to sending to the bank.

Minimal segregation of duties – the accounts receivable clerk opens the post alone and logs the cheques into the day book without any checks or verifications in place.

Payroll controls are weak because the wages clerk is able to make additional payments to the sales team member without any authorisation. She also has not verified the payment prior to making it in cash. There is also the potential that this has not been documented, and there is no evidence the sales team member has signed for the additional monies paid to him.

Health and safety regulations are not adhered to – an untrained person is using a forklift without having the relevant training. This may be an issue if there was an accident as it is likely that the company's insurance would be invalid.

The accounts receivable system is manual and there has been no regular review by management of the debt recovery process.

The company cheque book is not stored securely in a locked drawer or safe and so there is risk that it might be used inappropriately.

Activity 2: Logical controls

- Passwords
- Usernames
- Lists of who can and cannot access certain data
- Firewalls
- Encryption
- Multi-factor authentication
- Digital certificates

Logical controls are not the same as physical controls (so, for example, locking a PC away in a room may stop unauthorised access to that PC, but it is not a logical control).

Activity 3: Payroll risks

Risk assessment of the payroll system
There is a high risk of errors in the payroll system due to: • Unauthorised additional payments to staff taking place • New starters being put onto the system without any documentation regarding their hours, contract and terms and conditions, or whether they actually exist. • Large amounts of cash kept on the premises with staff being able to top up wages by taking £1,200 out of petty cash without any safeguards, checks or authorisation in place. • There being no controls over the hours and rates that staff are being paid. There is a risk that these could be amended resulting in staff being paid too much.

Risk of regulatory failure due to:

- New starters being paid on the system prior to the relevant tax information being received. There is a risk that their deductions will be incorrect, risking penalties from HMRC or complaints from staff affected.
- Spoilt payslips being thrown away and not correctly destroyed. This is a confidentiality risk and puts the company at risk of breach of data protection regulations.
- No checks on proof of identity are made, or references required when new staff members join. This could expose the company to risk of theft as well as breaches of money laundering regulations.

Risk of ethical breaches occurring in the workplace due to:

- Possible intimidation of payroll staff by the warehouse manager. All staff should be treated with respect; aggressive and threatening behaviour should not be tolerated.
- Breach of confidentiality by leaving spoilt payslips with employee information in the bin rather than being destroyed.

Activity 4: Inherent limitations of internal controls

The correct answers are:

Example	Human error ✓	Cost/benefit ✓	Fraud ✓	Non-routine ✓
Judgement can sometimes be faulty due to overconfidence, fatigue or stress	✓			
No matter how well designed or implemented an internal control is, there is a risk of the control not being able to cope with a random item				✓
Two or more parties work together to bypass the segregation of duties			✓	
A fund is set up to cover potential losses due to excessive insurance premiums		✓		
The results of an exception report are misinterpreted	✓			

Limitations of internal controls could occur in the following areas:

- **Human error** – human judgement can sometimes be faulty due to overconfidence, fatigue, stress etc. Such error can be traced back to either the design or implementation of a particular internal control.
  - Human error might be experienced in the **interpretation of results** from reports produced by the system of internal control (eg misinterpreting the results of an exception report).
- An entity may make a judgement on the amount of money that a control is designed to save, compared with the amount that such a control costs to implement (the so-called **'cost-benefit'** argument). For this reason, many entities do not arrange insurance cover for all their assets,

as the cost of such premiums would be prohibitive – instead, a fund is set up to cover potential losses.

- **Fraud** is one area already discussed where the limitations of internal control are very much exposed – **collusion** (where two or more parties work together to bypass the segregation of duties) can circumvent segregation of duties controls, while management can choose to ignore the controls in place due to the authority they hold over their employees.
- Finally, due to the **freak** or **non-routine** nature of some transactions, circumstances or events mean that no matter how well designed or implemented an internal control is, there is a risk of the control not being able to cope with such a random item. This can result in some form of loss for the entity, and may also highlight where an internal control can be improved.

Activity 5: Control objectives, risks and control procedures – introduction

Activity	Type
Financial statements contain inaccurate payroll information	Risk
Compare payroll costs with budget	Control procedure
Confirm a sample of payslips to timesheets and staff contracts	Control procedure
All pay and deductions should be accurately recorded	Control objective
Employees are paid for hours they have not worked	Risk
Employees should only be paid for hours they have worked	Control objective

Activity 6: Control objectives, risks and procedures for systems

Accounting systems – control objectives, risks and control procedures

Purchases

Control objective	Risk	Control procedures
Ordering		
A company should only order goods and services that are authorised by appropriate personnel and are for the company's benefit	The company pays for unnecessary or personal goods	• Orders should be authorised only when the need for the items has been justified (on a purchase requisition, for example) • Orders should only be prepared when authorised purchase requisitions are received from departments • Orders should be authorised by separate officers (segregation of duties) • Orders should be pre-numbered and blank order forms should be safeguarded • Orders not yet received should be reviewed
A company should only order from authorised suppliers	Other suppliers may not supply quality goods or may be too expensive	• A company should have a central policy for choosing suppliers

<table>
<tr><th>Control objective</th><th>Risk</th><th>Control procedures</th></tr>
<tr><td colspan="3">Receipt of goods and invoices</td></tr>
<tr><td>A company should ensure that goods and services received are used for the organisation's purposes</td><td>The company may pay for goods/services for personal use</td><td rowspan="4"><ul><li>Goods received should be examined for quality and quantity</li><li>Goods received should be recorded on pre-numbered goods received notes</li><li>Goods received notes should be compared with purchase orders by different staff (segregation of duties)</li><li>Supplier invoices should be checked to orders and goods received notes</li><li>Supplier invoices should be referenced (numerical order and supplier reference)</li><li>Supplier invoices should be checked for prices, quantities, calculations</li></ul></td></tr>
<tr><td>A company should only accept goods that have been ordered (and appropriately authorised)</td><td>The company may pay for goods/services for personal use</td></tr>
<tr><td>A company should record all goods and services received</td><td>The company fails to pay for goods/services and loses suppliers</td></tr>
<tr><td>A company should not acknowledge liability for goods it has not recorded</td><td>The company pays for goods it has not received</td></tr>
<tr><td>A company should ensure it claims all credits due to it</td><td>The company pays for poor-quality goods</td><td><ul><li>There should be procedures for obtaining credit notes from suppliers</li><li>Goods returned should be recorded on pre-numbered goods returned notes</li></ul></td></tr>
<tr><td colspan="3">Accounting</td></tr>
<tr><td>A company should only make authorised payments for goods that have been received</td><td>The company pays for goods it has not received</td><td><ul><li>Payments should be authorised and only made if goods have been received</li><li>The purchase ledger control account should be reconciled to the list of balances on a regular basis</li></ul></td></tr>
<tr><td>A company should record expenditure accurately in the accounting records</td><td>The financial statements are misstated, and the company does not pay for genuine liabilities</td><td rowspan="2"><ul><li>Purchases and purchases returns should be promptly recorded in day books and ledgers.</li><li>The purchase ledger should be regularly maintained</li></ul></td></tr>
<tr><td>A company should record credit notes received correctly in the accounting records</td><td>The financial statements are misstated, and the company pays for items unnecessarily</td></tr>
<tr><td>A company should record liabilities in the correct purchase ledger accounts</td><td>The company pays the wrong supplier</td><td><ul><li>Supplier statements should be compared with the purchase ledger</li></ul></td></tr>
</table>

Control objective	Risk	Control procedures
A company should record liabilities in the correct period	The financial statements are misstated by recording purchases but not inventory, or recording inventory but not the associated purchase liability	• Goods received but not yet invoiced at the year end should be accrued separately
Payment		
A company should only make payments to the correct recipients and for the correct amounts which are authorised	The company pays the wrong supplier	• Cheques should be requisitioned and requests evidenced with supporting documentation • Cheque payments should be authorised by someone other than a signatory • There should be limitations on the payment amount individual staff members can sign for • Blank cheques should never be signed • Signed cheques should be despatched promptly • Paid cheques should be collected from the bank (ie after the supplier has banked them, the company can get them back as proof)
A company should only pay for liabilities once	The company pays more than once and the supplier does not correct the error	• Electronic payments should be set up for payment and then separately authorised by another officer of the company (segregation of duties) • Electronic payment limits should be established through the banking software to ensure that large payments require at least two banking authorisations • The bank statement should be regularly reconciled to the cash book • Cash payments should be limited and authorised • Payments should be recorded promptly in the cash book and ledger

Revenue

Control objective	Risk	Control procedures
Orders and extending credit		
A company should only supply goods to customers who are likely to pay for them	Selling to customers who do not have a good credit rating	• Credit terms offered to customers should be authorised by senior personnel and reviewed regularly • Credit checks should be run on new customers • Changes in customer data (for example, their address) should be authorised by senior personnel • Orders should only be accepted from customers with no existing payment problems after confirming that those customers are within their existing credit limit • Order documents should be sequentially numbered so that false or missing sales can be traced
A company should encourage customers to pay promptly	The company loses the value of being able to use the money in their business or interest on the money in the bank due to late payment	
A company should record orders correctly	The company sends the wrong goods to the customer, causing added cost or risk of loss of the customer	
A company should fulfil orders promptly/in full	The company loses custom	
Despatching and invoicing goods		
A company should record all goods it sends out	Goods are sent out and not invoiced, and the company loses money	• Despatch of goods should be authorised by appropriate personnel and checked back to order documents (segregation of duties) • Despatched goods should be checked for quality and quantity • Goods sent out should be recorded • Records of sent out goods should be agreed to customer orders, despatch notes and invoices by separate staff (segregation of duties) • Despatch notes should be sequentially numbered and the sequence checked regularly • Returned goods should be checked for quality • Returned goods should be recorded on goods returned notes
A company should invoice all goods and services sold correctly	Insufficient sums are charged and the company loses money	
A company should only invoice goods it has sent out	The company charges for goods in error and loses custom	
A company should only issue credit notes where required	The company issues credit notes incorrectly and loses money	

Control objective	Risk	Control procedures
		• Customers should sign despatch notes as proof of receipt • Invoices should be prepared using authorised prices and quantities and should be checked to despatch notes • Invoices should be checked to ensure they add up correctly • Credit notes should be authorised by appropriate personnel • Invoices and credit notes should be pre-numbered and the sequence checked regularly • Inventory records should be updated from goods sent out records • Sales invoices should be matched with signed delivery notes and sales orders • Orders not yet delivered should be regularly reviewed
Recording and accounting for revenue, credit control		
A company should record all invoiced revenue in its accounting records, ie sales ledger and general ledger	Revenue is not recorded and wrongly omitted from financial statements, and payment is not chased as sale was never recorded	• Sales invoice sequence should be recorded and spoilt invoices recorded and destroyed • Sales receipts should be matched with invoices by separate staff (segregation of duties) • Customer remittance advices should be retained • Sales returns and price adjustments should be recorded separately from the original sale • Procedures should exist to record revenue in the correct period • Receivable statements should be prepared regularly • Receivable statements should be checked regularly • Receivable statements should be safeguarded so they cannot be amended before they are sent out • Overdue accounts should be reviewed and followed up • Write-off of irrecoverable debts should be authorised by appropriate personnel
A company should record all credit notes in its accounting records	As above, financial statements likely to be misstated and potential to lose custom by chasing cancelled debts	
A company should record all invoiced revenue in the correct sales ledger accounts	Losing custom by chasing the wrong customer for the debt and not receiving the money from the correct customer	
A company must ensure that invoices are recorded in the sales ledger in the correct time period	Errors in the financial statements due to counting both the sale and the related inventory as assets or counting neither	
A company must identify debts for which payment might be doubtful	The company fails to take action until it is too late to retrieve the debt and, in the worst case, wrongly records irrecoverable	

Control objective	Risk	Control procedures
	debts as assets in the financial statements	• The sales ledger control account should be reconciled regularly • The sales ledger and profit margins should be analysed regularly
Receiving payment (cash)		
A company should record all money received	Money could be stolen or lost, custom could be lost through chasing payments already made by the customer, the financial statements are likely to be misstated	• There should be safeguards to protect post received to avoid interception (segregation of duties) • Two people should be present at post opening, a list of receipts should be made and post should be stamped with the date opened (segregation of duties) • There should be restrictions on who is allowed to accept cash (cashiers or salespeople) • Cash received should be evidenced (till rolls, receipts) • Cash registers should be regularly emptied • Till rolls should be reconciled to cash collections which should then be agreed to bankings by separate staff (segregation of duties) • Cash shortages should be investigated • Cash records should be maintained promptly • There should be appropriate arrangements made when cashiers are on holiday • Receipts books should be serially numbered and kept locked up • Bankings should be made daily • Paying-in books should be compared to initial cash records • All receipts should be banked together • Opening of new bank accounts should be restricted and authorised • Cash floats held should be limited • There should be restrictions on making payments from cash received and restricted access to
A company should bank all money received	Money could be stolen or lost with consequences, as above, or the company loses out on interest that could be being made on receipts	
A company should safeguard money received in the period until it is banked	Money may be stolen in the interim period	

Control objective	Risk	Control procedures
		cash held on the premises • Cash floats should be checked by an independent person sometimes on a surprise basis • Cash should be locked up outside hours

Payroll

Control objective	Risk	Control procedures
Setting pay		
A company should only pay employees for work they have done A company should pay employees the correct gross pay, which has previously been authorised	The company overpays employees	• Personnel records should be kept; and wages and salaries checked to details held in them • Personnel files should be kept locked up • Engaging employees, setting rates of pay, changing rates of pay, overtime, non-statutory deductions from pay and advances of pay should all be authorised and recorded by separate staff members (segregation of duties) • Changes in personnel and pay rates should be recorded • Hours worked should be recorded; time should be clocked • Hours worked should be reviewed • Payroll should be reviewed against budget
Recording wages and salaries		
A company should record gross pay, net pay, and relevant deductions correctly on the payroll	The company may make incorrect payments to staff/tax offices and financial statements may be misstated	• Payroll should be prepared, checked and approved before payment
A company should record payments made in the cash and bank records and general ledger	The financial statements may be misstated	
A company should comply with the requirements of the Data Protection Act 1998	The company could make unauthorised disclosures of employee information	

<table>
<tr><th>Control objective</th><th>Risk</th><th>Control procedures</th></tr>
<tr><td colspan="3">Paying wages and salaries</td></tr>
<tr><td>A company should pay the correct employees</td><td>Angry, unpaid workforce and/or the company overpays the wrong people</td><td>• Wage cheques for cash payments should be authorised
• Cash should be kept securely
• Identity of staff should be verified before payment
• Distributions of cash wages should be recorded and undertaken by two employees (segregation of duties)
• Bank transfer lists should be prepared and authorised
• Bank transfer lists should be compared to the payroll</td></tr>
<tr><td colspan="3">Deductions</td></tr>
<tr><td>A company should ensure all deductions have been properly calculated and authorised</td><td>Breaking the law, calculating staff pensions incorrectly leading to staff displeasure</td><td rowspan="2">• Separate employee records should be maintained
• Total pay and deductions should be reconciled month on month
• Costs of pay should be compared to budgets
• Gross pay and total tax deducted should be checked to returns to the tax authorities</td></tr>
<tr><td>A company should ensure it pays the correct amounts to taxation authorities</td><td>Breaking the law and incurring fines</td></tr>
</table>

Inventory

<table>
<tr><th>Control objective</th><th>Risk</th><th>Control procedures</th></tr>
<tr><td colspan="3">Recording of inventory</td></tr>
<tr><td>Inventory movements authorised and recorded</td><td>Inventory might be stolen</td><td rowspan="4">• Segregation of duties between custody of inventory and recording
• Checking and recording goods inwards
• Issues of inventory supported by appropriate documentation
• Maintaining inventory records</td></tr>
<tr><td>Inventory records only include items that belong to the company or that exist at all</td><td>Inventory may be overstated in the financial statements</td></tr>
<tr><td>Inventory quantities have been recorded correctly</td><td>The company may have insufficient inventory to operate efficiently and inventory may be misstated in the financial statements</td></tr>
<tr><td>Inventory is not recorded as an asset once a sale has been made or before a purchase is recognised</td><td>The financial statements may be misstated</td></tr>
</table>

Control objective	Risk	Control procedures
Protection of inventory		
Inventory is protected from loss/damage	Goods might be stolen or unusable/unsaleable	• Restriction of access to stores • Controls on stores environment (temperature/damp etc) • Regular inventory counts by independent people • Reconciliation of inventory count to book records
Valuation of inventory		
Inventory is valued correctly	Inventory may be misstated in the financial statements	• Calculation of inventory value and checking of calculation • Regular review of inventory condition • Accounting for scrap and waste
Slow-moving, obsolete and damaged inventory is noted	Inventory may be overstated in the financial statements	
Inventory levels		
Levels of inventory held are reasonable	The company may not have sufficient inventory to function efficiently	• Maximum and minimum inventory levels set • Reorder limits set

Non-current assets

Control objective	Risk	Control procedures
Buying assets		
Non-current asset additions are authorised	The company buys assets it does not need and/or at an inappropriate price	• Capital expenditure is budgeted for/authorised by a senior official in the company (segregation of duties)
Storing and using assets		
Non-current assets are kept securely	The assets are stolen	• A non-current asset register is maintained and compared with actual assets and general ledger record of assets • Non-current assets are inspected regularly to ensure they are maintained/in use/secure
Non-current assets are maintained properly	The assets are not fit for use in the business when required	
Selling assets		
Non-current asset disposals are authorised	The company sells assets it needs to operate and/or at an inappropriate price	• Non-current asset sales or scrappage is authorised/ planned to avoid business interruption
Recording assets		
Non-current assets are properly accounted for	The company misstates non-current assets in the	• Rates at which depreciation is charged are authorised/checked

Control objective	Risk	Control procedures
and recorded	financial statements	• Non-current asset register is maintained
Rate at which depreciation is charged is reasonable	Assets are valued wrongly and financial statements are misstated	
Proceeds from disposal of non-current assets are recorded	Proceeds may be stolen or omitted from financial statements, profit or loss on sale of assets may be misstated in financial statements	

Cash and bank

Control objective	Risk	Control procedures
All cash should be held securely both in hand and at the bank	Cash is misappropriated through either fraud or error	• Controls to ensure the completeness of recording cash receipts • Post-opening procedures to ensure all remittances are complete (including segregation of duties) • Restrictions over who can receive cash, how they evidence cash receipts and regular reconciliations of receipts • Paying cash and cheques into the bank promptly • Reconciliation of funds received via electronic funds transfer at point of sale (EFTPOS) to ensure completeness • Physical controls over blank cheques and limited access to creating system-generated payments (such as BACS) • Petty cash controls (physical, authorisation, recording) • Cash flow forecasts and monitoring procedures to ensure cash needs are met
All receipts and payments should be recorded	Lack of visibility over transactions and balances	
Staff should be accountable for all cash transactions and balances	Transactions and changes to cash held and in bank accounts occur without authorisation	
The organisation should have the cash available that it needs	Being unable to pay bills as they fall due and incurring costs for having insufficient funds available	

Activity 7: Sales system fraud

(a)

Fraud which could occur at BCC Co	Why this risk has arisen
Stolen cash receipts through the non-reconciliation of the till records and the cash inside them	The risk is increased by leaving the tills full of cash overnight. Any error or shortfall will not be detected until the next day or when the staff come to reconcile the takings. Having significant amounts of cash on the premises increases the threat of theft or loss.
No credit check undertaken against B. Braithwaite	This is a potential fraud risk as the customer may buy items on credit with no intention of paying (theft of inventory) or the customer may be a fictitious one set up by an unscrupulous member of the sales team who wants to inflate their sales figures for commission payments.
Unallocated cash	Unallocated cash is a fraud risk. There is a risk that sales staff could have diverted funds from a customer and are using more recent cash receipts to try to cover this up, but there will always be a difference if the invoiced amounts do not match.
Writing off debts	All debts require management authorisation to be written off. Currently, debts are written off as and when the accounts receivable clerk believes that they cannot be collected or they have got 'just too old'.

(b) Without management or senior staff performing regular reviews of the aged receivables report, the following issues may occur:

Financial loss

The unallocated cash does not show what debts or final balances need to be settled by customers. By delaying the allocation of cash, it is possible that fraud could occur by 'teeming and lading' (cash receipts being skimmed off and then applying other customer receipts to cover it. By delaying the overall outstanding debt, this type of fraud may only appear if another person performs a reconciliation of the ledger or the customers are contacted directly).

Financial loss due to staff inflating the sales figures and earning more commission.

Financial loss due to inflated sales and risk of overstating VAT liability.

Non-financial

The high level of unallocated cash suggests that customers' invoices may appear to be outstanding when they have in fact been paid. This could adversely affect customer relations if they are chased for debts that they have settled in full.

Equally, with the cheques being dropped and lost when they are received in the post, the risk of paid debts being chased will affect customer relations.

If fraud has occurred, staff morale may drop due to a climate of suspicion.

Activity 8: Purchases system fraud

Ordering goods for own use – there are issues around segregation of duties between ordering, booking goods into inventory and making payments, plus appropriate authorisations. Management should authorise all purchase orders, so that all orders placed can be verified and there are no 'surprises' in value or in finding that staff are using company funds to purchase goods for personal use. Poor controls over the reconciliation of goods inwards also creates a risk that items may be taken from the warehouse without being noticed.

The potential for fictitious suppliers – there should be management authorisation of all new suppliers added to the system; reconciliation of payments to invoices; and some segregation of duties for these processes. The new suppliers may all be valid, but management should also be reviewing whether they represent best value in terms of price, quality and credit terms offered.

Invoices incorrectly calculated – BCC Co might have paid the incorrect amount of £15,000 if this had not been such a significant error and investigated further. Suitable controls would be to match GRNs to purchases orders, then match invoices to purchase orders when goods arrive to confirm that the supplier has correctly calculated the quantities and prices.

Time wasted – it took the senior accounts clerk all day to reconcile the manual system to find out what had happened with the incorrectly calculated invoice. If there was a fully integrated system, this would have been highlighted much sooner and any investigation would have taken significantly less time.

By delaying the payment to the supplier, and not raising the issue earlier, BCC Co has risked affecting the relationship with this supplier.

Cash flow effect – working capital would have been significantly affected if this £15,000 invoice had been paid, and there is the potential for strained relations with the bank if BCC Co had asked for an extension to its bank overdraft. Any request to increase the overdraft will result in higher interest charges, as well as possible arrangement fees.

Activity 9: Detecting fraud using financial information

- **Sales staff salaries** – have increased by 75% which, given the rise of revenue by 19%, is odd. There had been a case of one of the sales staff requesting additional commission and this being paid without being checked. This is a potential area of fraud. Sales commission should be reviewed by the directors prior to being paid. Management should be able to review the sales made by the member of staff (including any credits or refunds given). In order to ensure that credit notes are not being raised after the invoice in order to 'boost' sales, the commission should only be paid after a predetermined period of time (eg quarterly intervals) to allow cut-off testing to be performed.
- **Irrecoverable debts** – have increased by 175% (whereas revenue has increased by 19%). This suggests that there may be issues regarding the collection of cash or screening of customers (from Activity 7 we know B. Braithwaite was added with no credit checks). However, from a detection of fraud basis, this could also suggest that cash is being collected from customers and these debts are being written off rather than the cash being applied to them (there was lots of unallocated cash in the most recent aged receivables report). Irrecoverable debts which are written off should also be authorised by a member of management. Management should review a list of the debts (one of the directors last looked at it four months ago) to be written off with explanations as to why this is the case and steps taken to recover any outstanding debt.
- **Other costs** – management should ensure they understand what drives these costs so that they do not simply 'creep up' over time, as many of these should be fixed in nature.
- **Other factors which may be considered**
  - Ensuring that the management accounts are regularly reviewed by the management team
  - Monthly management accounts rather than quarterly would help to highlight any problems most quickly
  - Looking at the actual results against budget to see if the company is 'on track' and the accounts look reasonable

Test your learning

1 Complete the statement below describing a system of internal control.

Internal control is the process [▼], implemented and [▼] by [▼], [▼] and other personnel to provide [▼] about the achievement of the entity's [▼] with regard to the reliability of [▼], effectiveness and efficiency of [▼] and compliance with applicable laws and regulations.

Picklist

- Designed
- Financial reporting
- Maintained
- Management
- Objectives
- Operations
- Reasonable assurance
- Those charged with governance

2 Accounting systems have control objectives and control procedures to mitigate the risk that the control objective is not met.

Required

For each of the following, select whether they are a control objective, risk, or control procedure.

Activity	Type
A company should only pay for work done by employees.	▼
Company vehicles are used by employees for their own purposes.	▼
Part C39t99, in regular use in the business, is reordered when inventory levels fall below 200.	▼

Picklist

- Control objective
- Control procedure
- Risk

3 Select which one of the following statements concerning small and large companies is the least true by ticking the appropriate box.

	✓
Control activities will be similar in all sizes of company over core activities.	
A large company is likely to have a more formal control system than a small company.	
A small company is likely to have a less complex information system than a big company.	
A large company is more likely to have a good control environment than a small company.	

4 The personnel director at Metal Extrusions Midlands Limited (MEM) has contacted the audit firm and said that they want to overhaul the system of internal control over wages and salaries at MEM. All members of staff (waged and salaried) are paid by bank transfer. Waged staff members are paid weekly and salaried staff members are paid monthly. At present, the payroll is prepared and authorised by the personnel director, who has sole access to employee records. The bank transfer is authorised by the personnel director but enacted by the cashier.

Required

Set out the control objectives that the personnel director of MEM should consider when putting together a new control system for wages and salaries.

5 Listed below are two control procedures that the directors have put into action at MEM as a result of your recommendations.

Required

For each internal control procedure, use the picklist below to match the procedure with the control objective.

Internal control procedure	Control objective
The payroll should be reconciled to other records, such as the cash payment for net pay per the bank's records.	▼
The payroll should be authorised by someone other than the personnel director.	▼

Picklist

- Employees should only be paid for work done.
- Gross pay should be calculated correctly and authorised.
- Gross pay, net pay and deductions should be correctly recorded on payroll.
- Wages and salaries should be recorded properly in bank records.

6 An entity uses internal control procedures in order to mitigate the risk to which it is exposed. Listed below are two internal control procedures which are applicable to an entity's non-current assets system.

Required

For each internal control procedure, use the picklist below to match the procedure with the risk mitigated.

Internal control procedure	Risk mitigated
Non-current assets are inspected regularly.	▼
Capital expenditure is approved by the purchasing director on behalf of the board.	▼

Picklist

- Assets are bought from inappropriate suppliers at inflated cost.
- Assets are depreciated incorrectly.
- Assets are not maintained properly for use in the business.
- Assets are sold when they are needed for use in the business.

7 An entity uses internal control procedures in order to mitigate the risk to which it is exposed. Listed below are two internal control procedures which are applicable to an entity's inventory system.

Required

For each internal control procedure, use the picklist below to match the procedure with the risk mitigated.

Internal control procedure	Risk mitigated
Inventory store is kept locked.	▼
Goods inwards are checked for quality.	▼

Picklist

- Damaged inventory is valued in the financial statements.
- Inventory is counted in the financial statements without a corresponding payable.
- Inventory is stolen.
- The company fails to order required goods.

8 **What type of control activity is each of the following actions? Write your answer in the space provided.**

Action	Type of control activity
Person A matches dispatch notes to invoices; Person B creates invoice to customer	
Control account reconciliation	
Petty cash box kept locked	
Adequate resourcing of accounting function	
Review of budgetary control report	

9 **Identify for each of the following control activities which type of security control they are an example of.**

Activities	Type of security control
Validation of input data	▼
Passwords	▼
Encryption	▼
Archiving	▼

Picklist

- Integrity control
- Logical control
- Management control
- Physical access control
- Segregation of duties
- System control

10 **Complete the following statement:**

Management should regularly ensure that staff perform [▼] of the receivables ledger to ensure accuracy and completeness of the data.

Picklist

- Assessments
- Inspections
- Reconciliations
- Teeming and lading

11 **Complete the following statement:**

Control objectives in relation to taking orders and extending credit are part of the [▼] system of the accounting system.

Picklist

- Payroll
- Purchases
- Sales

12 **Complete the following statement:**

Completion of GRNs is a control activity related to the control objective of [▼].

Picklist

- Ensuring goods and services received are used for the company's purposes
- Only accepting goods and services that have been ordered and appropriately authorised
- Only accepting goods received that are of a sufficient quantity for the purposes of the organisation

- Recording all money received

13 Complete the following statement:

Allocating one customer's payment to another customer's account in order to balance the books and detract from a shortfall is called [▼] .

Picklist

- Identity fraud
- Inflation
- Reconciliation and review
- Teeming and lading

14 For each of the following situations where fraud is being discussed, identify the fraud triangle condition that is being described.

Situation	Fraud triangle condition
'They never check on the older items in the warehouse, so they are the easiest ones to steal.'	▼
'I have worked so hard for this company over the years and yet no-one notices. I am definitely entitled to take items out of the stationery cupboard for my own personal use.'	▼
'If I don't find the money in the next week, my house will be repossessed by the building society. I have to steal cash from the safe because I have no other way of finding the money I owe.'	▼

Picklist

- Dishonesty
- Opportunity
- Pressure
- Rationalisation

15 Identify the type of control being demonstrated in the activities below. Select the option from the picklist; some of the options may be used more than once or not at all.

Activities	Type of security control
Batch processing of invoices	▼
Only the finance manager can authorise new suppliers on the system	▼
Sequential numbering of invoices	▼
Alerts to the user when the journal being entered does not balance	▼

Picklist

- Completeness
- Integrity
- Processing

- Segregation of duties

16 An accounting system should meet the expectations and requirements of the organisation.

Required

Select the key objectives of the accounting system from the selection below.

Tick ALL that apply.

	✓
Cost effectiveness	
Ease of use	
Reliable	
Providing timely information	

17 Which TWO factors are evaluated to grade the risk of fraud in a fraud matrix?

	✓
Time	
Responsibility	
Likelihood	
Volatility	
Impact	

18 The THREE categories of impact of fraud on a company are:

	✓
Morale	
Social	
Reputation	
Environmental	
Financial	

19 Which of the following statements is correct?

	✓
During the analysis of the sales system, a fraud matrix graded the potential loss from misappropriation to be rated 5. Management have decided urgent action is required.	
A fraud matrix is a subjective analysis of an organisation's controls, and will ensure that all recommendations identified are actioned immediately.	
A control within the payroll system has been rated as 2 within the fraud matrix. Management have decided that this risk must be rectified immediately.	

2 The audit and assurance framework

Learning outcomes

2	**Understand the audit and assurance framework**
2.1	**The concepts and principles of audit and assurance** Learners need to understand: 2.1.1 the meaning of audit 2.1.2 the meaning of assurance 2.1.3 the audit expectation gap 2.1.4 the difference between reasonable and limited assurance 2.1.5 the difference between positive and negative expression of assurance 2.1.6 the benefits gained from assurance 2.1.7 the meaning of: • true and fair view • presents fairly • faithful representation as applied to the external audit 2.1.8 the importance of professional scepticism and professional judgement 2.1.9 that an external audit concludes with an audit report.
2.2	**The regulatory environment** Learners need to understand: 2.2.1 the approach to the regulation of audits in the UK 2.2.2 the use of audit standards in the UK 2.2.3 the role of the: • accountancy profession in the regulation of audits • International Auditing and Assurance Standards Board (IAASB) • International Sustainability Standards Board (ISSB) 2.2.4 the role of the Companies Act: • the requirement for a statutory audit • directors' responsibilities • auditors' responsibilities 2.2.5 that negligent misstatement is a form of negligence 2.2.6 the auditor's liability to: • the company • shareholders • third parties

	2.2.7 the requirement for professional indemnity insurance. **Excluded**: references to specific auditing standards
2.3	**The role of corporate governance in the audit and assurance process** Learners need to understand: 2.3.1 that the UK Corporate Governance Code contains the principles of: • board leadership and company purpose • division of responsibilities • audit, risk and internal control 2.3.2 the comply or explain principle 2.3.3 the responsibilities of management in relation to: • operational decisions • fraud and error • the financial statements 2.3.4 the responsibilities of internal and external auditors in relation to: • fraud and error • the financial statements 2.3.5 the importance of an effective audit committee.
2.4	**The role of internal audit** Learners need to understand: 2.4.1 the difference between internal and external audit 2.4.2 the benefits of internal audit 2.4.3 the functions of internal audit: • reviewing systems of internal control • conducting special investigations • reviewing compliance with external regulation • reviewing processes for value for money • reviewing the risk management process • reviewing sustainability practices 2.4.4 the risks associated with a lack of independence.

Assessment context

This topic introduces a number of terms that you will see examined as part of the *Audit and Internal Controls* assessment. The contents of this topic make up Task 4 in the assessment, so it is crucial that you understand the concepts discussed and how they could be examined.

Qualification context

Although there are some terms here that you may be familiar with from earlier parts of your AAT studies (such as sustainability and company law), you may need to consider the context in which they are examined.

Business context

While seen as an unnecessary expense for a number of organisations, the bureaucracy and 'red tape' attached to being incorporated and then audited can help to provide a degree of confidence to the many stakeholders of a company. This topic will start to address the confidence or assurance provided by auditors, especially when their ethical credibility has been reinforced by adhering to a code of ethics.

Chapter overview

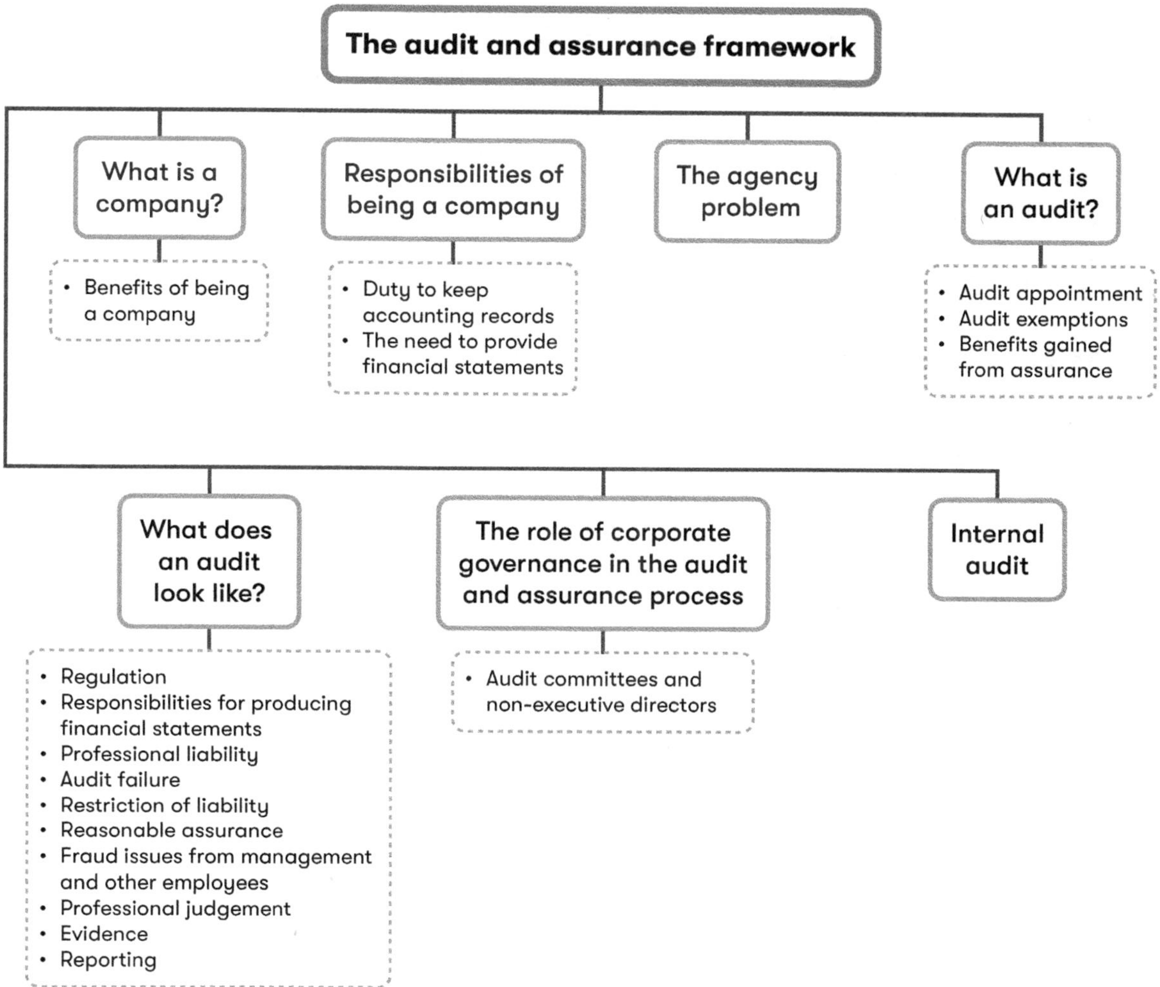

Introduction

We are going to start our journey through the audit and assurance framework by explaining why it is necessary in the context of a company's responsibilities to its stakeholders and the problems they face when getting proper visibility of their investment.

Within this chapter, we will learn what an audit is and how the concept of assurance can provide benefits to all those associated with a company. We will learn about regulatory issues such as corporate governance, liability, professional scepticism, and how the auditor starts to fulfil their responsibilities once appointed.

We will then move on to discuss Internal Audit and how it can help to increase the amount of trust placed in an organisation's systems. You will learn about what an internal auditor does and start to understand how they do it.

1 What is a company?

A company is an **organisation** set up ('incorporated') for a **specific purpose**, usually commercial. It is a separate legal entity and is registered under a piece of UK legislation called the Companies Act 2006.

A company may be viewed like this – a collection of related stakeholders:

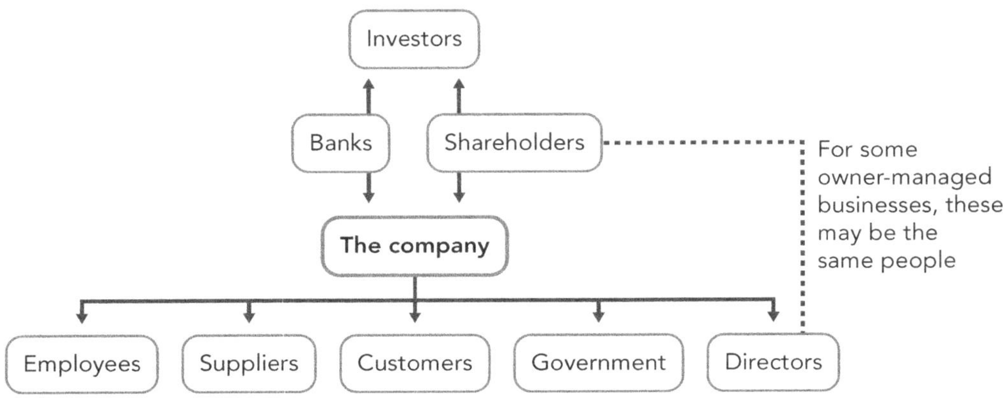

Registration under the Companies Act 2006 provides a company with specific **rights** but also forces upon it certain **responsibilities**, both of which we shall look at now.

1.1 Benefits of being a company

Companies are incorporated for many reasons. One of these reasons is the concept of **limited legal liability** where, in the event of any losses suffered by the company, the most that any investor can ever lose by being involved with that company is their investment. The company is consequently a separate legal entity from its shareholders.

2 Responsibilities of being a company

The Companies Act 2006 has over 1,300 different sections and covers over 750 pages of text, so a company's duties are **too numerous** to mention in full! However, there are two that are of particular interest to you for this course:

- The duty to keep **accounting records** (Companies Act 2006: s.386)
- The need to provide **financial statements** (Companies Act 2006: s.394)

2.1 Duty to keep accounting records

Section 386 of the Companies Act 2006 specifies the responsibilities of a company regarding the accounting records that must be kept.

Activity 1: Companies Act

Listed below are extracts from Section 386 of the Companies Act 2006.

(1) Every company must keep adequate accounting records.

(2) Adequate accounting records means records that are sufficient:

- (i) To show and explain the company's transactions
- (ii) To disclose with reasonable accuracy, at any time, the financial position of the company at that time, and
- (iii) To enable the directors to ensure that any accounts required to be prepared comply with the requirements of this Act (and, where applicable, of Article 4 of the IAS Regulation).

(3) Accounting records must, in particular, contain:

- (i) Entries from day to day of all sums of money received and expended by the company and the matters in respect of which the receipt and expenditure take place, and
- (ii) A record of the assets and liabilities of the company.

(4) If the company's business involves dealing in goods, the accounting records must contain:

- (i) Statements of stock (inventory) held by the company at the end of each financial year of the company
- (ii) All statements of stock-takings from which any statement of stock, as is mentioned in paragraph (a), has been or is to be prepared, and
- (iii) Except in the case of goods sold by way of ordinary retail trade, statements of all goods sold and purchased, showing the goods and the buyers and sellers in sufficient detail to enable all these to be identified.

Required

For each item highlighted above, suggest a suitable example or accounting record.

Section 388 of the Companies Act 2006 tells a company where and for how long such accounting records should be kept:

- In the case of a **private company (Ltd)**, for **three** years from the date on which they are prepared.

- In the case of a **public company (plc)**, for **six** years from the date on which they are prepared.
- A company's accounting records must be **kept** at its registered office or such other place as the directors think fit and must at all times be open to inspection by the company's officers and auditors.

2.2 The need to provide financial statements

The responsibility to provide financial statements creates an opportunity to address the concerns that certain investors might have.

Activity 2: Shareholder concerns

Consider the overview of a typical company. Assume that you represent the shareholders only and that the company's directors are not shareholders. What concerns might you have about them?

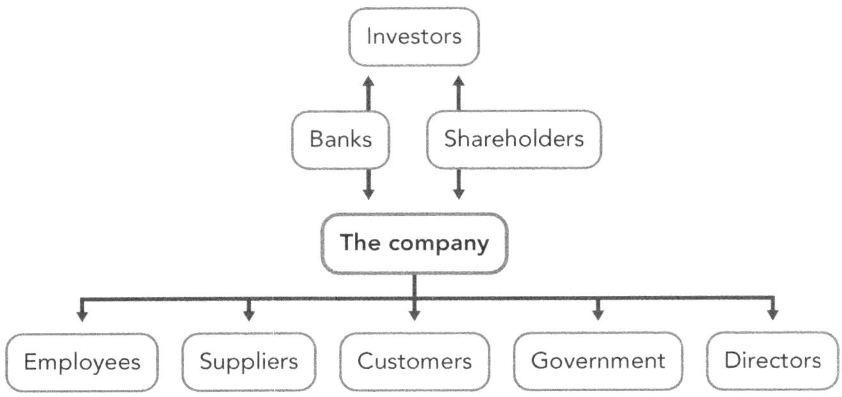

3 The agency problem

You already know from your AAT studies that the Companies Act requires **company accounts** to be produced – the logic of this seems more apparent now. **Forcing** company directors to produce **financial statements** goes some way towards alleviating shareholders' concerns over the **trust** and **visibility** issues raised as part of agency theory.

This is only **half the story**, though – we have seen plenty of examples of companies whose financial statements were misleading to the point of fraud (and beyond, taking **Enron** as a case in point). In some cases, financial statements can be misstated due to **unintentional error**, but what happens if directors attempt to cover their actions by **deliberately falsifying** the company's financial statements?

True and fair view (or presents fairly in all material respects)

KEY TERM

True and fair view: 'True' means honest and factual, while 'fair' means unbiased and free from discrimination.

Sometimes, the term 'presents fairly in all material respects' is used in the same way as 'true and fair view'. This has the same meaning as 'true and fair view' but is often preferred in jurisdictions outside the UK.

Faithful representation

In 2018, the **International Accounting Standards Board (IASB)** revised the *Conceptual Framework for Financial Reporting* (IASB, 2018), introducing the term 'faithful representation' as a fundamental qualitative characteristic of useful financial information. You will cover the Conceptual Framework in more detail in another unit. Faithful representation is defined as follows:

KEY TERM

> **Faithful representation:** Financial information represents the economic substance rather than the legal form, possessing the characteristics of completeness, neutrality and being free from error.
>
> **Complete:** All information necessary for understanding the phenomenon being depicted is present.
>
> **Neutral:** Without bias, supported by the exercise of prudence (prudence is the exercise of caution when making judgements under conditions of uncertainty).
>
> **Free from error:** Processes and descriptions are without error. This does not mean perfectly accurate in all respects. It just explains any issues that might affect accuracy, such as the need to present an accounting estimate of some kind.

(Conceptual Framework: paras. 2.12–2.15, 2.18)

The Companies Act puts in a **control** which is designed to **review** the **financial statements** and **supporting disclosures** and collect enough of the right kind of evidence to be able to conclude with some certainty that directors have been both **honest** and **factual** as well as **unbiased** and **free from discrimination** when reporting the company's position and performance. We will explore the idea of challenging the perception that directors should always be trusted when we discuss professional scepticism later in this chapter.

This control over financial statements is called the **external audit** and we will spend the rest of this unit looking at how auditors substantiate the terms 'faithful representation', 'true and fair view' and 'presents fairly in all material respects'.

4 What is an audit?

How does an **audit** address the agency problem? An external audit provides **assurance** to those who need it, which in this case is those stakeholders who rely on the financial statements of a company.

KEY TERM

> **Audit:** An audit is an independent review of the financial statements and disclosures produced by directors to ensure that they are both true and fair.
>
> **Assurance:** Assurance is a degree of confidence that is provided by a practitioner when reviewing subject matter produced by a responsible party for the benefit of the intended users of that subject matter. Assurance can be expressed in different ways and to different extents.

The external audit

The statutory audit used as a solution to the agency problem is referred to as an external audit. This is different to internal audit which you will learn more about later in this chapter. For now, we will refer to the external audit as just an audit, but it is important that you can tell them apart.

Illustration 1: Assurance engagements

The following diagram illustrates a typical assurance engagement:

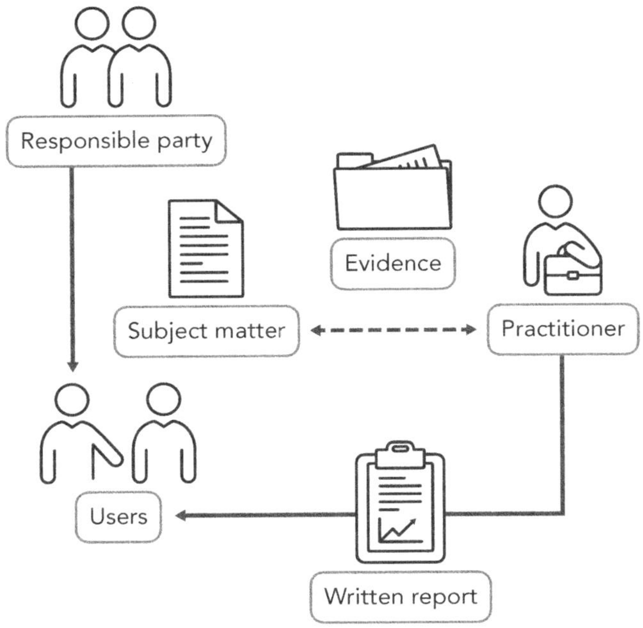

Practical uses of assurance:

- Audits
- Internal control reports
- Reviews of business plans
- Sustainability and corporate social responsibility reports
- Reviews of management performance via KPIs, adherence to voluntary codes etc

Activity 3: Assurance engagements

Assume that the following diagram represents an audit as an example of an assurance engagement – fill in the boxes with the options from the picklist to describe how the audit would work.

Required

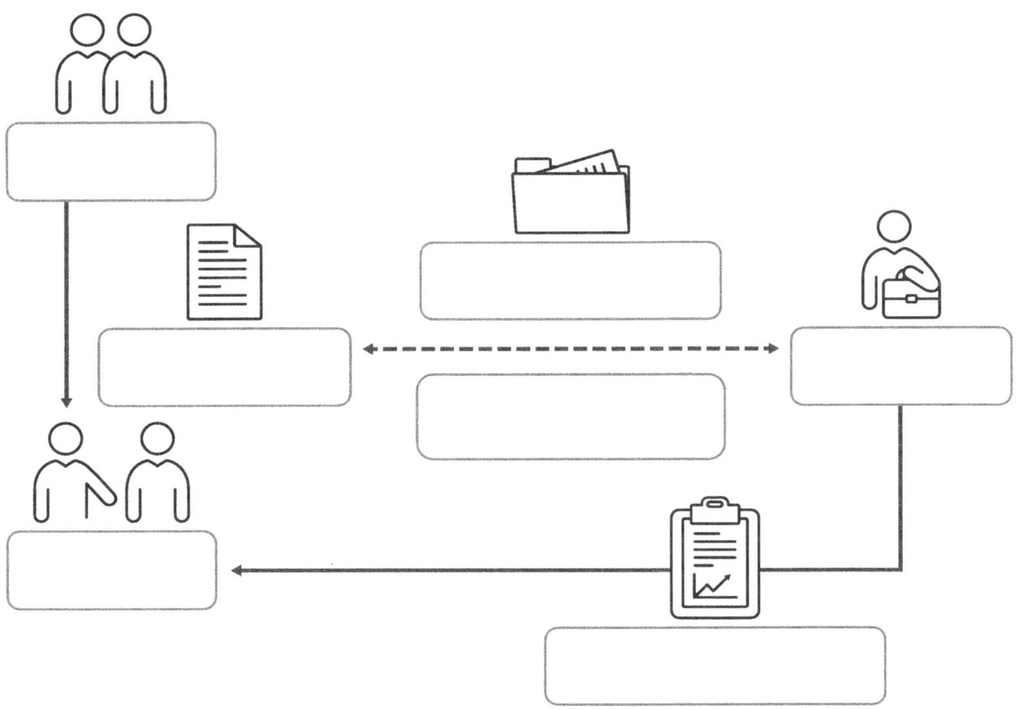

Picklist

- The criteria = Auditing, accounting and other standards
- The evidence = Outcome of sampling and testing
- The practitioner = External auditor
- The report = Auditor's report (including their opinion)
- The responsible party = Directors
- The subject matter = Financial statements
- The users = Shareholders

4.1 Audit appointment

Auditors are usually appointed by shareholders at an **Annual General Meeting** (AGM) but can be appointed by directors in certain circumstances (such as the date of incorporation, or if the existing auditors resign and replacements need to be appointed before the next AGM). Auditors are usually **re-elected annually** at the AGM but in private (Ltd) companies that happens automatically unless they are removed by shareholders or they resign (Companies Act 2006: s.485).

4.2 Audit exemptions

While the external audit provides valuable **assurance** to **many stakeholders** and acts as a **deterrent against fraud and error**, as a process it can be **expensive, time consuming** and **inconclusive**. In the event of a company being **owner-managed** (as suggested by the diagram above) the benefit of being provided with an assessment of one's own work can also have limited value.

As a result of these issues, the Companies Act 2006 allows for some companies to be **exempt** from both full reporting and audit requirements, although some information is still required by Companies House.

To qualify for the audit exemption, a company has to satisfy **at least two of the following requirements for two consecutive years**:

- Turnover (revenue) of not more than £15 million during the year
- Balance sheet total (statement of financial position) of not more than £7.5 million
- Not more than 50 employees

(Open Government Licence v3.0, 2024)

The audit exemption **cannot** be claimed if a company falls into one of the following:

- A public, or listed, company (plc)
- A bank or insurance company
- A company that is part of a group of companies that are public companies, banks or insurance companies.

Dormant companies (those which have not recorded any transactions within the relevant accounting period) are also exempt from audit provided: they are not a bank or insurance company; they are not required to produce group accounts; and they fulfil two of the three criteria above. However, they can be a plc (Companies Act 2006, s.477–481).

4.3 Benefits gained from assurance

Despite the cost and disruption associated with the audit, and the fact that owner-managers may feel they have no agency problem to address, many companies that are exempt from audit still choose to have one – why do you think this is?

- There is obvious value from having an independent, qualified accountant **review the business** including its financial records and systems (including the staff it employs and the technology it relies upon).

- It **satisfies external stakeholders** such as banks and shareholders that the business is operating satisfactorily.
- It can act as a **deterrent** against the threat of **fraud** occurring in the business.
- The business may **grow** to levels beyond the exemption threshold one day so getting used to an audit now makes it less difficult to have one in the future.

Now that we know why people have audits, we will look in more detail at what an audit actually is and how it is done, including the various forms of report that can be used to provide the assurance offered by the auditor.

5 What does an audit look like?

An audit helps to provide the required **assurance** via its report to shareholders by following a series of procedures laid down by **auditing standards** known as International Standards on Auditing (ISAs). You will not need to be familiar with the detail of these ISAs but it is still important that you understand the basic concepts they contain. We will therefore start with the basic contents of an audit and consider some useful terminology.

Overall Objectives of the Auditor

In conducting an audit of financial statements, the overall objectives of the auditor are:

(a) *To obtain reasonable assurance about whether the financial statements as a whole are free from material misstatement, whether due to fraud or error, thereby enabling the auditor to express an opinion on whether the financial statements are prepared, in all material respects, in accordance with an applicable financial reporting framework; and*

(b) *To report on the financial statements, and communicate as required by the ISAs, in accordance with the auditor's findings.*

(ISA (UK) 200: para. 11)

5.1 Regulation

We mentioned earlier that shareholders need visibility and trust – this is where the auditor comes in. An audit is designed to provide credibility in the financial statements of an entity and is presented in the form of an **opinion** that the financial statements either **present fairly in all material respects** or **give a true and fair view** (both of these are acceptable) of the financial position, performance and prospects of the entity.

The auditor uses whatever the **applicable financial reporting framework** is for that entity and jurisdiction – this is sometimes called GAAP (Generally Accepted Accounting Principles) supported by the relevant auditing standards and other standards where applicable. The audit opinion is communicated to shareholders in a specific way using an auditor's report (you will see what this includes in a later chapter).

KEY TERM

International Audit and Assurance Standards Board (IAASB): This is an independent body, part of the **International Foundation for Ethics and Audit (IFEA)**, which sets international standards on auditing that apply across multiple jurisdictions.

Financial Reporting Council (FRC): The independent regulator of the accounting and auditing professions in the UK. The Government has delegated responsibility for standard setting to the FRC as well as quality inspections, corporate governance and disciplinary action across the accountancy profession.

Audit, Risk and Governance Authority (ARGA): This body is expected to replace the FRC and will have more wide-ranging powers following a series of recent regulatory reforms in the UK. The creation of ARGA was included in the King's Speech to Parliament in 2024 but no further details have been issued by the Government, so for the purposes of your assessment, you can assume that the relevant standard-setting body in the UK is the FRC.

International Sustainability Standards Board (ISSB): The ISSB is responsible for developing international sustainability standards that will result in a high-quality, comprehensive global baseline of sustainability disclosures focused on the needs of investors and the financial markets. The ISSB supports the creation of globally comparable information on sustainability-related risks and opportunities for the purposes of investment decision-making.

Note. While the information produced using ISSB standards may be useful to auditors, these standards are not relevant to an audit of financial statements.

The ISAs set by the IAASB have been adopted by the UK's FRC as national requirements in the UK. The IAASB is an independent standard-setting body that **serves the public interest** by setting high-quality international standards for auditing, quality management, review, other assurance, and related services. These standards are used in more than 130 jurisdictions to enhance the **quality and uniformity of audit** and assurance engagements and strengthen public confidence in markets and economies (IAASB, 2026).

New standards are researched and consulted on, then subjected to public debate. The resulting draft standards are exposed to the public for comment. Any comments arising are considered and acted upon if necessary. A new standard is then issued when a majority of the IAASB's members approve it.

The ISAs contain objectives, requirements and application and other explanatory material to help an auditor obtain reasonable assurance. The auditor must follow the requirements of relevant ISAs and must also understand the whole text of an ISA to enable requirements to be applied properly.

5.2 Responsibilities for producing financial statements

The financial statements of an entity are produced by the **management** and **those charged with governance** of entity as part of their responsibilities under the Companies Act 2006.

KEY TERM

Those charged with governance: The directors of a company who are responsible for managing the company on behalf of the shareholders.

Are there any responsibilities that apply to **auditors?** We know that ISAs must be followed by auditors when undertaking an audit of a set of financial statements, but **what else** must the auditor consider? Here are some examples:

- Laws (such as the UK Companies Act 2006)
- Regulations (such as the UK Corporate Governance Code, covered later in this chapter)
- Case Law (such as that relating to professional liability)

5.3 Professional liability

As we know, the audit is an exercise carried out for the benefit of the shareholders of a company, as the ultimate output is the **auditor's report** which is addressed to them. It enhances the **confidence of users** to know that the directors have put together financial statements that are free from material misstatement.

If the **auditors** give a **poor service**, that is if they perform an audit that is of substandard quality (for example, which states there are no material misstatements in the financial statements when there are), they may be **liable to the shareholders** as a result. Performing a poor-quality audit may constitute **negligence** under English law, which is a matter for the courts to decide.

KEY TERM

Negligence: The way in which a service is carried out (ie carelessly) and the legal wrong which arises when a person breaks a legal duty of care that is owed to another and causes loss to that other.

For negligence to be proven, three separate things must be established:

(a) The fact that a duty of care existed

(b) The fact that this duty of care was breached

(c) The fact that this caused loss to the claimant

These requirements are further explained below.

(a) **Duty of care**

Under English law, auditors owe a duty of care to their client. The **duty of care** is a legal obligation to meet a required standard of care towards another party. This duty is implied into the **contract** between an auditor and a client and cannot be disputed. Therefore, in negligence cases, if the claimant is the client with whom the audit firm has a contract, point (a) above needs no further proof.

In the case of auditors, this is slightly complicated by the question of who the client is.

We have noted above that the audit is conducted for the benefit of shareholders.

However, in English law, the shareholders of a company are often not considered in isolation; that is, as individuals, but as a single body. In that context, the shareholders are described as being the company.

Shareholder
Shareholder
Shareholder
Shareholder
Shareholder

The company

It is the **body of shareholders**, known as the company, that is considered to be the client for the purposes of negligence in audit.

When the body of shareholders (the company) as a whole sues for negligence, point (a) above does not have to be proven.

The situation is different if an individual shareholder or another third party sues for negligence.

The audit is primarily carried out for the shareholders. However, other parties may be interested in the financial statements of a company. In most companies, the following parties may be interested.

- The **bank** (often a major lender to the company)
- **Suppliers** (who may extend credit to the company)
- **Customers** (who rely on the company to provide a quality service)
- **Employees** (who rely on the company for income)
- **Tax authorities** (who want to levy the correct tax from the company)
- If the company is public limited, **potential investors** (who are considering whether to invest in the company)
- **Individual investors** (who might want to increase or decrease their stake in a company).

While all these parties may be interested in the audited financial statements, it is important to remember that the audit is not carried out for their benefit. They are not the client, and **English law has historically substantially restricted the chances of these parties proving the auditors owed them a duty of care.**

One reason for this is that, in the case of these parties, the auditor **does not automatically owe them a duty of care**, and they would **have to prove that one existed**.

The way that a duty of care **might** exist is **if these parties have constructed a relationship with the auditors**, for example by:

- Warning them that they believe a duty of care exists; or
- Telling them they are relying on the audited financial statements for a special purpose.

However, even then, **it is not automatic**, and the auditors may be able to disclaim liability to these parties and say that a duty of care did not exist. Then **the courts will have to decide whether such a duty did exist, examining the facts.**

(b) **Breach of duty of care**

For all parties, not only does a duty of care have to exist, but the claimant must also prove that this **duty was breached**.

Again, this is a matter for the courts to determine when presented with the facts. However, there are some generally accepted principles about auditing which may indicate whether a duty of care has been met or breached.

For example, it is generally accepted that auditors will conduct audits according to professional standards. You should bear in mind that if an audit firm does not carry out audits according to these professional standards, it may make it easier to prove that a duty of care has been breached by the firm.

(c) **Loss caused**

This is the third item that needs proving in a case of negligence. The claimant will have to show not only that they have suffered a loss, usually a financial loss, but also that the **loss was as a result of the breach of the duty of care on the part of the auditors**. Again, this will be determined by the courts.

If the auditors are found to have been negligent, they may have to pay financial reparation (known as **damages**) to the claimant.

Activity 4: Duty of care

Select whether the auditors owe a duty of care to the following parties using the picklist options.

Party	Duty of care owed?
Company	▼
Bank	▼
Individual shareholder	▼
Creditor	▼

Picklist

- Automatic
- Must be proved
- Never

5.4 Audit failure

KEY TERM

Audit failure: Performing a poor-quality audit resulting in the auditors being found guilty of negligence can be described as audit failure, which can have serious consequences for audit firms.

One such consequence of audit failure has already been mentioned. A firm may have to pay out substantial **damages** to a claimant if it has been proven that the auditors were negligent. This would clearly adversely affect the audit firm, and may even cause it to cease to operate, if the damages were so sizeable as to bankrupt the firm.

Such a legal case against a firm would bring substantial bad publicity, impacting on the firm's ability to retain and engage clients in the future, even if they did continue to operate.

In addition, audit firms have supervisory bodies that monitor their activities (in the UK, that is the FRC). The FRC might take **disciplinary action** against the firm and its partners in the event of negligence, which could result in its ability to conduct audits being suspended.

5.5 Restriction of liability

KEY TERM

> **Liability limitation agreement:** An agreement between an auditor and their client that limits the amount of auditor liability in the event of any negligence.
>
> **Proportional liability:** Where a professional firm agrees to be liable for only a share of any damages due to a client on respect of negligence or other litigation.

The Companies Act 2006 entitles auditors to negotiate liability limitation agreements with their clients. The effect of such agreements is to restrict the amount of damages to be paid in the event that negligence is proved against them. This restriction may be a specified amount above which an auditor will not be liable (a **liability cap**) or an agreement that, if there are other parties contributing to the loss and the damage, the auditor will only be held liable for his portion of the damage (**proportional liability**) (Companies Act 2006: s.534).

There are other ways that auditors can restrict their liability. Many firms include a statement in their auditor's report specifically **excluding liability** to parties other than the shareholders. This is known as a Bannerman paragraph, after the legal case in which such a course of action was recommended for auditors to avoid liability to third parties.

Individual audit **partners can limit their personal liability** for the firm's debts from such matters by changing how the audit firm is legally formed.

Traditionally, audit firms have been partnerships, where each partner is liable for the debts of the firm jointly with the other partners. Now, many audit firms are set up as a limited liability partnership (LLP), where the **partners collectively have limited liability** in the same way that shareholders in a company do. There are some drawbacks to forming an LLP, however: for example, the requirements for increased publicity, such as filing accounts with the Companies Registrar.

Lastly, a firm is likely to insure against professional liability by taking out **professional indemnity insurance**. In practice, **audit firms are required to do this by their supervisory body** in the public interest, so that if a firm is found liable, the injured parties can be compensated.

5.6 Assurance

The opinion given by the auditor is just that – an **opinion** – and is not a guarantee. There are virtually no guarantees in life and although the auditor's work is thorough, it is **impossible** to review every single transaction and balance in a set of financial statements, so absolute assurance is not possible. We also stated previously that systems of internal controls can also never be 100% foolproof due to **inherent limitations** in every system. Consequently, the auditor has to base their opinion on evidence that is **persuasive** rather than conclusive. So, does that mean that the audit opinion is worthless?

Auditing standards require the auditor to perform procedures that provide **reasonable assurance** that the financial statements are free from **material misstatement** due to either **fraud or error**. The extent of these procedures is such that the auditor is required to obtain **sufficient appropriate audit evidence** to reduce the risk they give an incorrect opinion to an **acceptably low level**. Consequently, the assurance that is given is high but not absolute. Such **reasonable assurance** is expressed in **positive terms**:

> 'In our opinion, the financial statements give a true and fair view of the company's affairs.'

Audit firms can undertake **activities other than audits** (such as a review of a set of forecasts in support of a bank loan, or interim review of figures to be supplied to the stock market) where the level of assurance given can never be as high as that given for an audit due to the inherent uncertainties involved (ie predicting the future) or the extent of evidence collected (interim figures are required quickly, so procedures cannot be as thorough as they would be for an audit). This level of assurance is referred to as **limited assurance** and is communicated in **negative terms** – here is an example of what this might look like:

> 'Based on the work undertaken, nothing has come to our attention to suggest that the forecast is misstated and that the underlying assumptions are unreasonable.'

The implication from this is that if more work were done, the level of assurance that could be given would be higher and reasonable assurance provided. Limited assurance engagements often consist of enquiries and analytical procedures – you will learn more about these in a later chapter when the audit approach is discussed further.

To summarise:

Assurance level	Communicated	Example
Reasonable	Positive	'In our opinion, the financial statements give a true and fair view...'
Limited	Negative	'Based on the work we have done, nothing has come to our attention...'

Audit expectation gap

KEY TERM

Expectation gap: This term is used to describe the difference between the expectations of those who rely upon an auditor's report concerning the audit work they think should be performed and the actual work performed by the auditor.

The expectation gap arises due to a general **misunderstanding** by the **public** of the **respective responsibilities of both management** and the **auditor**, and a **misunderstanding** of the **scope of an audit**. Such misunderstandings might include the following perceptions:

- It is the auditor's duty to prevent and detect all fraud at an audit client
- The auditor is liable for any errors found in the financial statements

To **counter** these perceptions and reduce this gap, regulators have attempted to address these **misunderstandings** by improving the **layout** and **language** of the auditor's report to clarify the work done by both auditors and management (for example, the auditor's need to obtain only reasonable, not absolute, assurance).

Activity 5: Types and levels of assurance

Identify whether the following sentences display a type of assurance or an expression of assurance and, for each one, select the most appropriate description from the picklist below:

Statement	Description
'In our opinion, the financial statements present fairly, in all material respects...'	▼
This is provided as part of the auditor's opinion and is classed as high, but not absolute.	▼
This is not provided for an audit as it is only moderate and is insufficient for an audit.	▼
'Based on our review, nothing has come to our attention that causes us to believe that the financial statements are presented unfairly, in all material respects...'	▼

Picklist

- Limited assurance
- Negative expression of assurance
- Positive expression of assurance
- Reasonable assurance

5.7 Fraud issues from management and other employees

We learned in the previous chapter that fraud is a **deliberate** attempt to gain an unjust advantage, usually by some form of deception

As stated above, an audit is not explicitly designed to uncover fraud – the **primary responsibility** for preventing and detecting fraud rests with those charged with the governance of an entity, and management. When we looked at a company's control environment, we saw that it is primarily through internal controls that a company tries to prevent fraud.

However, an **auditor** is still responsible for detecting material misstatements which may have arisen due to fraud. The inherent limitations discussed earlier (such as evidence being **persuasive**, rather than conclusive) are particularly significant in relation to a fraud which people are making a **deliberate attempt to hide**. It may be even more difficult to detect management fraud than employee fraud because management may be able to manipulate financial records themselves. It is therefore very important for auditors to deploy professional scepticism and to be alert to identifying opportunities for fraud to take place.

KEY TERM

> **Professional scepticism:** An attitude that includes a questioning mind, being alert to conditions which may indicate possible misstatement due to error or fraud, and a critical assessment of evidence. Auditors should be prepared to challenge such conditions as required.

Many of the auditing standards use the term '**professional scepticism**' on numerous occasions to alert the auditor to the dangers of placing unrealistic levels of **trust** in both the management and other staff employed by the entity being audited. To combat this, the Companies Act 2006 (s.507) states that if an employee of the company knowingly or recklessly gives the auditors a false or deceptive statement they are guilty of a criminal offence.

From the **inherent limitations of internal controls** to the **risks associated with giving an audit opinion**, this seems more and more likely to revolve around not just errors but also **fraud**, so auditors need to remember that the risk of material misstatement through fraud is increased when the auditor is sceptical of management's **attitude** and/or **integrity**.

The term '**money laundering**' covers most aspects of fraud, including the following:

- Offences that indicate dishonest behaviour – such as tax evasion or not returning overpayments by customers (where the client has attempted but failed to return such overpayments, dishonesty is not indicated)
- Offences that involve saved costs (such as where a company is saving money by not complying with environmental law; for example, by dumping waste illegally rather than paying a company to remove it)
- Conduct overseas that would be illegal in the UK - for example, bribery of government officials

The **Proceeds of Crime Act 2002** sets down responsibilities for auditors to inform the **National Crime Agency (NCA)** of any suspicions they may have regarding money laundering – they must not alert the suspect, though, as 'tipping off' is classified as a crime as well (Proceeds of Crime Act 2002, s.333).

Activity 6: Fraud risk and professional scepticism

Consider the following situations that have occurred during an audit:

- The finance director has requested that you complete the audit on time in order to meet head office reporting deadlines. The finance director has a profit-related bonus but has always accepted adjustments that you asked for on previous audits.
- The payroll officer has asked that you do not perform any testing of the payroll until she returns from her holiday. There are no other members of staff who can assist you with the payroll audit.
- When reviewing the board minutes, you read that the company has applied for significant funding to support the currently poor cash flow. From recent conversations with the chief

accountant, however, you were under the impression that revenue and cash flow were both healthy and that the company was performing well.

Required

For each of these situations, explain whether they would be likely to cause the auditor a greater or lesser degree of professional scepticism.

How do auditors make sure they don't miss any occurrences of fraud?

Auditing standards provide some examples of **fraud risk factors** for auditors to be alert to using the main conditions that contribute to fraud occurring, split between misappropriation of assets and fraudulent financial reporting:

Fraudulent financial reporting

Incentives/pressures

- Financial stability/ profitability is threatened
- Pressure on management to meet the expectations of third parties
- Personal financial situation of management threatened by the entity's financial performance
- Excessive pressure on management or operating personnel to meet financial targets

Opportunities

- Significant related-party transactions
- Assets, liabilities, revenues or expenses based on significant estimates
- Domination of management by a single person or small group
- Complex or unstable organisational structure
- Internal control components are deficient

Attitudes/rationalisations

- Ineffective communication or enforcement of the entity's values or ethical standards by management
- Known history of violations of securities laws or other laws and regulations
- A practice by management of committing to achieve aggressive or unrealistic forecasts
- Low morale among senior management
- Relationship between management and the current or predecessor auditor is strained

Misappropriation of assets

Incentives/pressures

- Personal financial obligations
- Adverse relationships between the entity and employees with access to cash or other assets susceptible to theft

Opportunities

- Large amounts of cash on hand or processed
- Inventory items that are small in size, of high value, or in high demand
- Easily convertible assets, such as bearer bonds, diamonds, or computer chips
- Inadequate internal control over assets

Attitudes/rationalisations

- Overriding existing controls
- Failing to correct known internal control deficiencies
- Behaviour indicating displeasure or dissatisfaction with the entity
- Changes in behaviour or lifestyle

The auditing standards also provide some examples of **circumstances that may indicate the possibility of fraud**:

- Discrepancies in accounting records (eg incomplete, unusual or unsupported transactions)
- Conflicting or missing evidence (eg inventory items, altered documents, unexplained items and vague or implausible responses from management)
- Difficulties in the relationship between the auditor and management (eg delays in providing evidence, intimidating behaviour from management and even denial of access to certain aspects of the audited entity's records or systems)
- Unwillingness to allow the auditor access to those charged with governance
- Unusual accounting policies that are at odds with the rest of the industry or sector

(FRC, 2025a)

To assist the auditor in **responding appropriately to fraud risks and other factors**, auditing standards recommend a series of audit procedures that could be used, split between those at the assertion level and those misstatements that again relate to both fraudulent financial reporting and the misappropriation of assets:

Assertion level	• Surprise visits to locations subject to audit inspection • Alteration of the audit approach from year to year • Investigating manual adjustments and others that appear significant or unusual • Making use of automated tools and techniques to analyse data • Reviewing the use by the client of a management's expert (someone in possession of skills outside of accounting, such as a surveyor or legal expert) to determine the appropriateness of their work
Fraudulent financial reporting	• Corroborating revenue by confirming amounts recognised with customers • Attending inventory counts without any prior notice • Using an auditor's expert to corroborate any accounting estimates created by management

Misappropriation of assets	• Counting cash and/or assets as close to the year-end as possible to prevent the risk of manipulation • Making use of automated tools and techniques to verify payroll amounts, inventory balances and sales discounts • Analysing vendor lists and comparing them with payroll to identify potential supplier-based frauds • Analyse expense reports submitted by senior management for appropriateness

Note. The terminology in use here will be covered in more detail later in the course when we cover how auditors obtain audit evidence.

5.8 Professional judgement

We know that the audit contains inherent limitations and that the opinion given can only ever contain reasonable assurance at best. The auditor needs to display sound **professional judgement** when determining the approach that will be taken given the finite time and resource available during the course of the audit.

One of the key areas where the auditor displays professional judgement is the use of **materiality** – we mentioned earlier that reasonable assurance does not indicate that the financial statements are free from all misstatements, just misstatements that are material. We will define 'material' in a later chapter when we discuss how the auditor evaluates risk, but at this point, you can assume that **materiality is a measure of how important something is to the financial statements.** It is evaluated in both quantitative and qualitative terms and guides the auditor when deciding what they should and should not be looking at during the audit.

However, although the auditing standards provide illustrative examples of what might be considered material, it is always based on the professional judgement of the auditor relative to the circumstances of the audit.

5.9 Evidence

The terms **professional scepticism** and **professional judgement** are again relevant here to reinforce the alertness required by the auditor when obtaining sufficient appropriate levels of audit evidence.

Obtaining evidence is how the auditor reaches a conclusion and forms their opinion – we will look at ways of obtaining evidence in a later chapter. The Companies Act 2006 assists auditors by giving them a **right of access at all times** to all the company's books, accounts and vouchers and to require all company officers to supply whatever information and explanation they feel is necessary for the audit.

Professional scepticism includes learning to tell when things may not be as they appear, even when interviewing clients and documenting such discussions, while **professional judgement** dictates what gets prioritised and the approach that should be taken.

5.10 Reporting

Once all of the evidence has been collected, the auditor reviews it all and forms a conclusion over what they have discovered. We already know there is a statutory duty to report the findings of the audit, but what other forms of communication are required?

The auditing standards require the auditor to report two things at the conclusion of a statutory audit:

- A summary of any **deficiencies in internal controls** that have been identified during the course of the audit

  This information is designed to show what was identified by the auditor during the course of the audit. It is reported to management and those charged with governance along with conclusions from their findings and recommendations for rectifying any issues (although it is not the same as any work that the company being audited might perform as part of their own monitoring and review work).

- A summary of the **main findings of the audit** reported to those charged with governance

  This is a formal communication of the matters that those charged with governance need to know – in addition to confirming the work that has been done, this includes how the audit was conducted and the main audit findings.

It is worth pointing out that in relation to their **money laundering responsibilities**, the auditor may decide not to communicate certain matters to anyone at the company if doing so would be considered tipping off (in such cases, they would be more likely to escalate this by informing either a regulatory body or other authorities as required).

Finally, the **auditor's report** contains a number of elements that you will learn more about later in this unit, but in summary it looks like this:

- A title and a suitable addressee
- The auditor's opinion on the financial statements (true and fair/presents fairly)
- An explanation of the basis for that opinion, including a description of the scope of the audit
- Issues related to the audited entity's going concern, key audit matters from the audit and other information (these are not all required for every audit, though)
- Responsibilities of both auditors and management for the financial statements
- Regulatory issues for the jurisdiction concerned
- The auditor's signature, address and date that the report was signed.

6 The role of corporate governance in the audit and assurance process

KEY TERM

Corporate governance: The system by which companies are directed and controlled (FRC, 2024).

Corporate governance attempts to address the agency problem we discussed earlier by introducing transparency and accountability into the way that directors run a company.

Using the 2024 edition of the **UK Corporate Governance Code** as an illustration, areas typically covered by corporate governance include the following:

The principles of board leadership and company purpose

A. A successful company is led by an effective and entrepreneurial board, whose role is to promote the long-term sustainable success of the company, generating value for shareholders and contributing to wider society.

B. The board should establish the company's purpose, values and strategy, and satisfy itself that these and its culture are all aligned. All directors must act with integrity, lead by example and promote the desired culture.

C. Governance reporting should focus on board decisions and their outcomes in the context of the company's strategy and objectives. Where the board reports on departures from the Code's provisions, it should provide a clear explanation.

D. In order for the company to meet its responsibilities to shareholders and stakeholders, the board should ensure effective engagement with, and encourage participation from, these parties.

E. The board should ensure that workforce policies and practices are consistent with the company's values and support its long-term sustainable success. The workforce should be able to raise any matters of concern.

The principles of the division of responsibilities

F. The chair leads the board and is responsible for its overall effectiveness in directing the company. They should demonstrate objective judgement throughout their tenure and promote a culture of openness and debate. In addition, the chair facilitates constructive board relations and the effective contribution of all non-executive directors, and ensures that directors receive accurate, timely and clear information.

G. The board should include an appropriate combination of executive and non-executive (and, in particular, independent non-executive) directors, such that no one individual or small group of individuals dominate the board's decision making. There should be a clear division of responsibilities between the leadership of the board and the executive leadership of the company's business.

H. Non-executive directors should have sufficient time to meet their board responsibilities. They should provide constructive challenge, strategic guidance, offer specialist advice and hold management to account.

I. The board, supported by the company secretary, should ensure that it has the policies, processes, information, time and resources it needs in order to function effectively and efficiently.

The principles of audit, risk and internal control

M. The board should establish formal and transparent policies and procedures to ensure the independence and effectiveness of internal and external audit functions and satisfy itself on the integrity of financial and narrative statements.

N. The board should present a fair, balanced and understandable assessment of the company's position and prospects.

O. The board should establish and maintain an effective risk management and internal control framework, and determine the nature and extent of the principal risks the company is willing to take in order to achieve its long-term strategic objectives.

The Code also covers the **appointment** and **succession** of suitable board members and how their **performance** is appraised, plus **remuneration policies** that align the interests of the board with the long-term success of the company. (FRC, 2024)

One of the ways in which transparency can be demonstrated by directors is the publication of a set of **audited financial statements**. In a jurisdiction that adopts a **principles-based** approach, such as the UK, directors are required to adopt a principle known as **'comply or explain'**.

KEY TERM

Comply or explain: A company can either comply with the requirements of the Code, or they must explain how and why they have not complied, which provides flexibility and supports a more informed judgement for anyone relying on the audited financial statements.

You will learn more about the role of the **internal auditors** later in this chapter, but in summary, they support the management of a company by helping to address a number of issues including, but not limited to, the preparation of the accounting records, and ultimately, the financial statements. It is the job of the **external auditor** to review the financial statements and produce an auditor's report which contains their audit opinion on truth, fairness and faithful representation.

However, taking the UK as an example, you should remember that the external audit is first and foremost a **legal requirement**. **However**, to satisfy the **regulatory requirements** of the stock market and other investors, the external audit is also seen as a way of **supporting strong corporate governance**.

6.1 Audit committees and non-executive directors

One of the underpinning elements of corporate governance is the use of **non-executive directors**. These are directors who only sit on the board and therefore have no other day-to-day responsibilities within the company, which means they can be used to **evaluate** the **performance** of executive directors **without any concerns over their objectivity**.

In order to evaluate both **internal** and **external audit** as well as the **financial statements**, the board will form an **audit committee staffed only by non-executive directors**.

KEY TERM

> **Audit committee:** A collection of non-executive directors charged with overseeing various controls in place over the audited financial statements.
>
> **Non-executive director:** A board member whose responsibility it is to evaluate the effectiveness of the financial reporting process.

Taking the UK Corporate Governance Code (FRC, 2024) as an example, the audit committee consists of three or more non-executive directors (two for smaller companies) one of whom should have recent and relevant financial experience. The audit committee is **responsible** for the following:

- Monitoring the **integrity** of the financial statements of the company and any formal announcements relating to the company's **financial performance**, and reviewing significant financial reporting **judgements** contained in them;
- Providing advice (where requested by the board) on whether the annual report and accounts, taken as a whole, is **fair, balanced and understandable**, and provides the information necessary for shareholders to assess the company's **position and performance, business model and strategy;**
- Following the guidance in the separate FRC document **Audit Committees and the External Audit: Minimum Standard** (see below);
- Reviewing the company's **risk management** and **internal control framework**, unless expressly addressed by a separate board risk committee composed of independent non-executive directors, or by the board itself;
- Monitoring and reviewing the effectiveness of the company's **internal audit function**, or where there is not one, considering annually whether there is a need for one and making a recommendation to the board;
- **Reporting to the board** on how it has discharged its responsibilities.

In summary, the non-executive directors on the audit committee are responsible for **reviewing the audited financial statements** produced by the executive directors. This makes them an **effective** control in addressing the **agency problem**.

Audit Committees and the External Audit: Minimum Standard

In May 2023, the FRC published additional guidance for audit committees which focuses on the following four areas:

(a) **Responsibilities**

In addition to those responsibilities set out in the UK Corporate Governance Code, the Minimum Standard advises audit committees on their responsibilities for tendering, external audit appointments (including ethical issues, non-audit services, fees and scope), inviting challenge from the external auditor and ensuring the external audit is effective and has been conducted in line with professional and regulatory requirements.

(b) **Tendering**

It is the audit committee's responsibility to support competitive and transparent tendering for its external audit based on quality, independence, challenge and technical competence. Those entities that are required to follow the Code must retender for their audits every 10 years and rotate their auditors every 20 years.

(c) **Oversight of auditors and audit**

The audit committee is responsible for the external audit being an effective process. This is achieved via a mindset or culture that supports quality (including those risks to quality being achieved), challenge, independence and objectivity, accountability and stakeholder feedback.

(d) **Reporting**

An entity's annual report should communicate the significant matters that the audit committee considered during the external audit (and how they were addressed) plus issues relating to the independence, tenure, quality and competence of the audit and details of any disagreements between the board and the audit committee in relation to appointment, removal or reappointment.

(FRC, May 2023)

7 Internal audit

KEY TERM

> **Internal audit:** An independent control designed to evaluate and improve the effectiveness of governance, risk management and control processes in an organisation.

We have already mentioned the role that internal audit plays in both **corporate governance** and **internal control**, but you will also need to understand some **other aspects** of internal audit.

You will remember that the **audit committee** is responsible for all aspects of the organisation's auditing requirements, and this includes an overall determination of the **requirement for internal audit** within an organisation. Let's look at some governance best practice for guidance on this.

Factors that could influence **the need for internal audit** within a business include:

- The company's **size** or **complexity**
- Unexpected **risk** events or perceived **problems** in **internal control**
- A **cost vs benefit** approach - would it save more money than it costs?

The UK Corporate Governance Code also says:

> 'The annual report should describe the work of the audit committee, including [...] where there is no internal audit function, an explanation for the absence, how internal assurance is achieved, and how this affects the work of external audit [...].'

Consequently, it may therefore be helpful to **compare and contrast** the work that internal audit does with that of the **external auditor**. We know that external audit is primarily an examination of the accounting records of an organisation with a statutory goal of reporting on the truth and fairness, or faithful representation, of the organisation's **financial statements.** How does that compare with the work of **internal audit** then?

	Internal audit	External audit
Reports to	Management	Shareholders
Responsible for	Any task required by management or directors	Opinion on truth and fairness and compliance with laws and regulations
Activities undertaken	Anything	Testing via evidence gathering
Standards used	Anything	Laws and regulations Auditing standards Accounting standards

Despite the statutory aspects of having an **external audit**, it is actually a very **narrowly defined** activity when compared with the work that the internal auditor might be asked to perform. The **roles that internal audit could play in an organisation are many and varied** and can be illustrated by the following list:

- **Reviewing accounting** and **systems of internal control** – this could include work on **systems** such as revenue, purchases or payroll, as well as **management audits** where the performance of management in some capacity is evaluated to determine its effectiveness
- Examining **financial operating information** – this could include work that is either **financial** (such as profitability) or **operational** (such as achieving a particular goal or target)

- **Special investigations**, such as **fraud** (both prevention and detection)
- **Project work**, including social or environmental reviews – the scope of such work is very broad and will depend on the organisation, but it could consider **social factors** such as working conditions for staff or **environmental matters**, such as establishing the organisation's carbon footprint
- Reviewing **compliance** with **external regulation** which you might see operating within industries such as petrochemicals or financial services
- Reviewing **value for money (VFM)**, which is often associated with **public sector organisations** (demonstrating that public money has been wisely and responsibly spent) but which can also be applied to any organisation keen to **make the most of its finite resources**
- **Risk management**, where the internal auditor participates in some or all of the process of managing risk within an organisation (such as identifying situations where risk is more likely to occur, and then quantifying those risks in order to determine the most appropriate action to be taken)
- Internal auditors may also be used to **review sustainability practices in place** within an organisation (either to identify risks and opportunities in line with the ISSB methodology or to evaluate performance against criteria that have been set by the entity or using an external framework)

Despite their differences, **external auditors** may also use the work and skills of **internal audit** to reduce the work they need to perform during an external audit, such as performing testing on systems of internal controls and other parts of the business. However, this will only happen if the internal audit function is considered **effective**, which would include an overall assessment by the audit committee of whether internal audit is able to **achieve the objectives** it has been set.

In order to evaluate the **effectiveness of internal audit**, the **audit committee** must also consider the overall **objectivity** and **independence** of **internal audit**. This could be **adversely affected** by issues such as:

- A **lack of authority** among internal audit staff who are unable (or unwilling) to challenge management (poor quality procedures and practices could also undermine the internal audit function's perceived authority)
- **Involvement in the implementation of systems** that internal audit may ultimately be asked to review
- **Familiarity** with staff who work at the same organisation (this is exacerbated by appointing existing operational staff to work within internal audit)

A lack of independence could **compromise** the extent or effectiveness of any work undertaken, so care must be taken by the audit committee to establish appropriate **reporting** and **operating conditions** for internal audit to be considered an effective part of internal control.

Reporting is taken care of by making the internal audit function **responsible to the audit committee** and not to anyone in an operational capacity. To assess **operating conditions**, we could use auditing standards which explain that the internal auditors will be evaluated by the external auditors when deciding whether their work can be relied upon by the following **criteria**:

- The extent to which their **organisational status** and **relevant policies and procedures** support their **objectivity**
- Their level of **competence**
- Whether they display a **systematic and disciplined approach**, including **quality control** (FRC, 2024).

Chapter summary

- Companies are legal entities that are set up for a specific purpose and have many different stakeholders (investors such as banks and shareholders, plus employees and directors, customers and suppliers and the government which is interested in keeping all parties happy!).
- Companies have many responsibilities: in the UK they are laid out by the Companies Act 2006 which specifies two areas for this unit: (i) keeping adequate accounting records and (ii) providing financial statements.
- Due to the differences between owners and directors of a company, there can be a lack of visibility and trust over the truth and fairness (or faithful representation) of the company's financial statements, which leads to something called the agency problem: this can be overcome by the financial statements being subject to an independent review which is known as an audit.
- Audits are carried out by qualified professionals who are appointed to provide a degree of credibility for the work done by directors in running the company on behalf of the investors who own it. This credibility is called 'assurance'. Not all companies require an audit but there can be benefits from having one voluntarily.
- International Standards on Auditing (ISAs) provide a framework for audits carried out all across the world – these are created by the International Auditing and Assurance Standards Board (IAASB) and in the UK are adopted and regulated by the Financial Reporting Council (FRC). The International Sustainability Standards Board (ISSB) is responsible for standards that support the publication of sustainability information relevant to financial decisions. Sometimes an expectation gap exists, which highlights the differences between what some people think an audit is supposed to do and what the auditor actually does.
- Many responsibilities exist for both managers and auditors of companies subject to audit – included in these are an awareness of what happens when an audit fails due to auditor negligence and the techniques used by auditors to control such failures.
- Auditors are expected to collect enough evidence during the audit to be able to provide an appropriate amount of assurance for their opinion (either reasonable assurance expressed in a positive manner, or limited assurance expressed in a negative manner). Part of this evidence gathering requires auditors to be alert to the threat of fraud such as money laundering: to combat this and other frauds, auditors are encouraged to display 'professional scepticism' in order to apply their judgement appropriately.
- The auditor will communicate the findings of the audit to a variety of stakeholders, including shareholders, those charged with the governance of an entity and regulators, and will do so in a specific manner using an auditor's report.
- One possible solution to the agency problem is the adoption of corporate governance practices, which see the appointment of non-executive directors to the board of a company in order to review the quality of the audited financial statements. They will sit on an audit committee which is also responsible for addressing issues such as internal audit, risk management, internal control and all things related to the external auditor.
- To support sound systems of internal control within corporate governance best practice, internal audit functions are used to ensure that other internal controls have been designed and are operating appropriately. Internal audit also performs a variety of other activities to support an organisation (such as special investigations, value for money studies, sustainability reviews or risk management).

Activity answers

Activity 1: Companies Act

Accounting records for transactions:	Income statement/Statement of profit or loss/Statement of profit or loss and other comprehensive income/Statement of cash flows
Accounting records for financial position:	Balance sheet/Statement of financial position
Matters in respect of which the receipt and expenditure takes place:	Revenue (including invoicing details of customers) Purchases (as above, with invoices for suppliers) Payroll (including employee records) Stock (inventory) Investment
Assets and liabilities:	Property, plant and equipment Vehicles Trading licences Cash Stock Provisions Loans Overdrafts
Statements of stock held by the company:	Results from stock count at warehouse, factory, third parties etc (raw materials, work in progress (WIP), finished goods etc)

Activity 2: Shareholder concerns

Concerns about the directors of your company could be many and varied (such as 'Will they do a good job?', 'Could we have appointed someone better?' and 'Is our money safe?') but in broad terms, the concerns you have could be summed up by two phrases:

(1) **Visibility** – as owners of the company, we employ directors for their entrepreneurial skills and their ability to make money, which is better than our own; hence their appointment. However, in order to allow them to concentrate on this, we must leave them alone to run and manage our company as they see fit. Decisions are taken and events occur without us being involved, meaning that we cannot always see how directors behave. This leads to the second concern:

(2) **Trust** – without any visibility of directors' actions and decisions, until the resultant outcomes become apparent, we must simply trust them to be doing the right thing.

These issues of trust and visibility are known as the **agency problem** – where agents (directors) are employed by principals (shareholders), there is always a risk that each party's interests might not be properly aligned and the company does not behave in the way intended by shareholders.

Activity 3: Assurance engagements

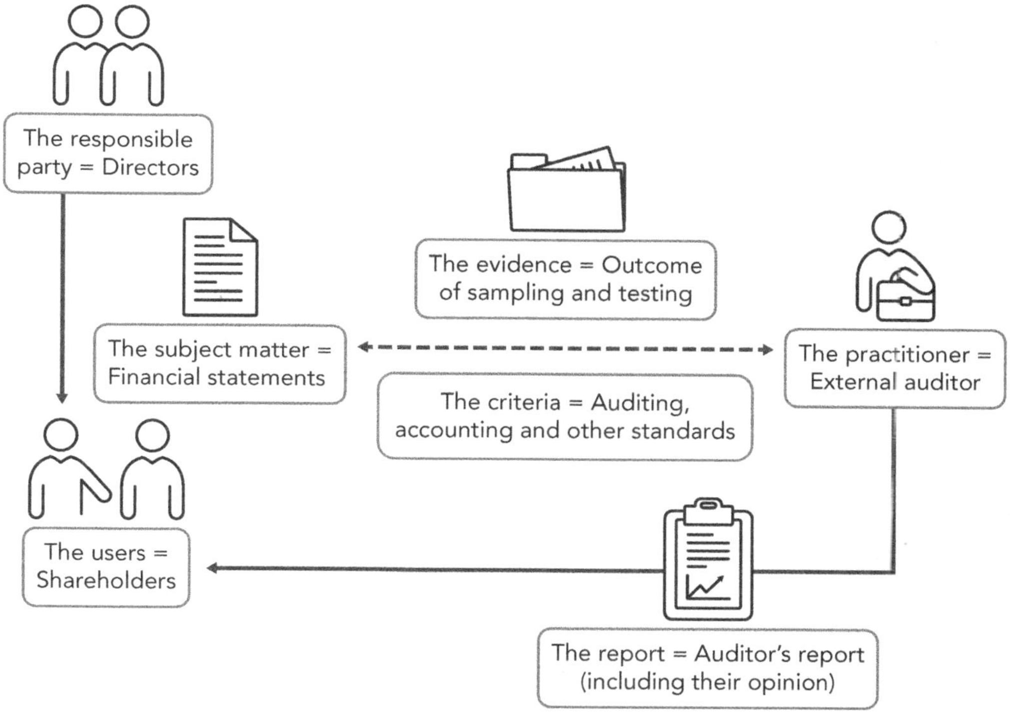

Activity 4: Duty of care

Party	Duty of care owed?
Company	Automatic
Bank	Must be proved
Individual shareholder	Must be proved
Creditor	Must be proved

The auditors do owe a duty of care to the client; that is, the shareholders as a body (the company) automatically under UK law. It is always possible that they may also owe a duty of care to other parties, such as the bank, individual shareholders and creditors, if those parties have established a special relationship with the auditors.

Activity 5: Types and levels of assurance

Statement	Description
'In our opinion, the financial statements present fairly, in all material respects…'	Positive expression of assurance
This is provided as part of the auditor's opinion and is classed as high, but not absolute.	Reasonable assurance
This is not provided for an audit as it is only moderate and is insufficient for an audit.	Limited assurance
'Based on our review, nothing has come to our attention that causes us to believe that the financial statements are presented unfairly, in all material respects…'	Negative expression of assurance

The amount of work undertaken by auditors allows them to deliver reasonable assurance, expressed in a positive manner ('In our opinion…').

Other engagements (such as reviews) do not collect the same amount and quality of evidence as audits, so can only deliver limited assurance, which is a lower level of assurance than reasonable assurance. Consequently, these are expressed in a negative manner ('Based on our review, nothing has come to our attention…').

Activity 6: Fraud risk and professional scepticism

	Greater professional scepticism?	Lesser professional scepticism?
The finance director has requested that you complete the audit on time in order to meet head office reporting deadlines. The finance director has a profit-related bonus but has always accepted adjustments that you asked for on previous audits.		There is always a risk of managers trying to influence profit figures to increase their bonus, but this seems to be reasonable and does not add to your sense of scepticism.
The payroll officer has asked that you do not perform any testing of the payroll until she returns from her holiday. There are no other members of staff who can assist you with the payroll audit.	Such a case is classic fraud-masking behaviour. The fraud can be perpetrated and kept secret by one member of staff while they are present and kept secret while they are away, as no one will be looking at their work. This is evidence of a poor control environment as well, so casts some doubt on the integrity (or at least competence) of management.	
When reviewing the board minutes, you read that the company has applied for significant funding to support the currently poor cash flow. From recent conversations with the chief accountant, however, you were under the impression that revenue and cash flow were both healthy and that the company was performing well.	Such an oversight is not likely to be a simple accident, more likely an attempt to mislead the auditor – again, this is a symptom of a poor control environment and shows the integrity of management in a poor light.	

Test your learning

1 Select which one of the following statements is not an implication of registering a company by ticking the appropriate box.

	✓
It is seen as distinct from its owners.	
It is required to have an audit, unless exempt.	
It must keep accounting records.	
It must be managed by its owners.	

2 Complete the following definition of an audit.

A(n) [▼] is an exercise carried out by [▼] to ascertain whether the [▼] prepared by the [▼] are (in the UK) in accordance with UK GAAP and the [▼] and give what is known as a(n) [▼].

Picklist

- Audit
- Auditors
- Companies Act 2006
- Directors
- Financial statements
- True and fair view

State whether the following statements are true or false in respect of external auditors' duties and rights.

Statement	True or false?
Auditors are required to report on the truth and fairness of financial statements.	▼
Auditors have a right of access to a company's books and records at any time.	▼
Auditors are entitled to obtain explanations from the officers of a company.	▼

Picklist

- False
- True

4 Select which one of the following best describes to whom the auditors owe a duty of care by ticking the appropriate box.

Auditors owe a duty of care to:

	✓
All users of financial statements	
The client (that is, the company, comprising all the shareholders)	
Shareholders	
The client and any other parties with whom they have implied a special relationship	

5 Set out what three things need to be proven in a case for negligence.

6 The UK Corporate Governance Code specifies certain criteria for the composition of an audit committee.

Required

Which TWO of the following audit committees satisfy the requirements of the Code?

	✓
Company A is a small company that is unlisted but has voluntarily chosen to introduce an audit committee of two non-executive directors	
Company B is a listed entity which has an audit committee consisting of four non-executive directors where recent and relevant financial experience is provided by the finance director	
Company C is a small company that is also a bank so has opted not to have an audit committee	
Company D is a listed entity that has an audit committee consisting of three non-executive directors	

7 The UK Corporate Governance Code uses a specific principle to describe how relevant information should be presented by companies.

Required

Which TWO of the following are the terms used in the Code?

	✓
Apply	
Explain	
Comply	
Report	

8 During the audit of Sneaky Ltd, the audit senior discovered a file of invoices which did not appear to be included in the financial records, for which the company has been paid in cash. No VAT has been paid in relation to these sales.

Required

Select which one of the following is the most appropriate action for the audit senior to take by ticking the appropriate box.

Report the matter to:

	✓
The board of directors	
HMRC	
The audit firm's money laundering reporting officer	
All of the above	

9 **Select which one of the following best describes who undertakes the role of monitoring controls at a company by ticking the appropriate box.**

	✓
Controls are always monitored by an internal audit function, as this is the purpose of their existence.	
Controls are monitored by the directors of a company.	
Controls are monitored by the people who operate them, as they are in the best position to assess whether the objectives of the controls are being met.	
Who monitors controls depends on the size of the company and its personnel: it may be an internal audit function, but it could also be the directors, or department heads.	

3 Planning and risk assessment

Learning outcomes

Having studied this chapter, you will be able to:

3	**Understand the planning and risk assessment process for audit engagements**
3.1	**The concept of audit risk** Learners need to understand: 3.1.1 components of the audit risk model: • inherent risk • control risk • detection risk: - sampling - non-sampling 3.1.2 how auditors manage detection risk 3.1.3 the factors that affect inherent risk and control risk 3.1.4 how analytical procedures can be used to identify potential understatement or overstatement of items in the financial statements 3.1.5 that misstatements in the financial statements can arise from either fraud or error 3.1.6 the two types of fraud that are relevant to the auditor: • misstatements resulting from fraudulent financial reporting • misstatements resulting from misappropriation of assets. Learners need to be able to: 3.1.6 identify audit risks 3.1.7 identify analytical procedures that could expose understatement or overstatement of items in the financial statements.
3.2	**The concept of materiality** Learners need to understand: 3.2.1 the difference between performance materiality and materiality for the financial statements as a whole 3.2.2 the role of materiality in planning an audit and evaluating misstatements 3.2.3 methods used to calculate materiality thresholds 3.2.4 the difference between material and material and pervasive.

Assessment context

This topic supports Task 5 in the assessment which will probably feature multiple sub-requirements, so you need to ensure you understand all aspects of this topic.

Qualification context

You will by now be starting to see some familiar terms such as those used in previous chapters but this is the first time you will have seen audit risk and materiality in such detail.

Business context

The 21st century auditor needs to consider the risks associated with their chosen profession. Although this chapter focuses on overall audit risk, there are plenty of other risks that the auditor faces on a regular basis – reputation, commercial and litigation risks, to name but three.

Chapter overview

Planning and risk assessment

- **Understanding the entity**
  - Financial statement level
  - Assertion level
- **Audit risk**
  - Inherent risk
  - Control risk
    - Client factors
  - Detection risk
    - Auditor driven
    - Sampling risk
    - Non-sampling risk
- **Analytical procedures**
  - Profitability
  - Operating ratios
  - Gearing
- **Materiality**
  - Calculations:
    - 5–10% Profit before tax
    - 1–2% Revenue
    - 2–5% Total assets
  - Material but not pervasive or Material and pervasive?
  - Performance materiality

Introduction

In order to plan the audit in an effective manner, the auditor needs to consider those areas that are most likely to present **possible misstatements** in the financial statements and **prioritise the audit approach** accordingly. How can the auditor **identify** these high-risk areas?

It starts with risk assessment and an understanding of what is called **audit risk**, which needs to take a number of factors into account – the things that could go wrong, what the audit client can do about them, and how the auditor responds to such matters.

To assist the auditor in making a more informed choice about risks, there are techniques that can help with this prioritisation. You may have already met **analytical procedures** before, but we will take a look at how they can help to understand the messages locked inside the numbers in the financial statements. We also need a way of understanding the point at which something starts to become significant, and this is called **materiality**. Hopefully, you are starting to see some of the terms we have already covered in a way that makes the audit seem more connected.

1 Understanding the entity

We have already seen how auditing standards provide guidance on how to conduct an audit, but in order to **understand the entity** being audited, there is another aspect that you need to know about which helps the auditor to **plan** an **effective** audit and deliver their **audit opinion**:

KEY TERM

> **Risk assessment procedures:** Audit procedures designed to identify and assess the risks of material misstatement whether due to fraud or error, at both financial statement and assertion level.

The definition above mentions risks at **two levels**, each of which could influence the opinion given by the auditor:

- The **financial statement level** – there is a possibility that certain factors might have a detrimental effect on the **whole set of financial statements**. For example, flaws in the control environment, an overall lack of management integrity or competence or even **adverse economic conditions** could lead to the entire set of statements being affected.
- The **assertion level** – there may only be **one specific element** of the financial statements that is at risk of material misstatement due to problems with one or more **characteristics** of that element. For example, if **material assets** listed on the statement of financial position are **incorrectly valued**, there is a **material misstatement** in respect of them due to the **assertions made by management about their value**. We will look at assertions in more detail later.

The auditing standards list the **circumstances** that should be considered as part of an entity's risk assessment process, using categories that include **complexity**, **subjectivity**, **change**, **uncertainty** and the **susceptibility to misstatement as a result of fraud or management bias**:

- Changes in the operating environment (regulatory or even competitive)
- New personnel within an organisation
- New or revamped information systems
- Rapid growth
- New technology
- New business models, products or activities
- Corporate restructurings
- Expanded foreign operations
- New accounting pronouncements

(FRC, 2025b)

The external auditor therefore faces a **serious problem** when agreeing to deliver an audit opinion – in the same way as any **critic** might be at risk when asked for their opinion, this could easily be **discredited** if it has not taken into consideration all available **information** and the auditor's **expertise**. How does the auditor make sure such information and expertise has been taken into consideration? The answer lies in **understanding the risks** faced by auditors and **working to control them** by use of the **audit risk model**.

2 Audit risk

KEY TERM

Audit risk: The risk that the auditor does not detect one or more of the risks that relate to an audit and gives an opinion that the financial statements are true and fair when, in reality, they are materially misstated in some way due to incorrect and/or inappropriate accounting or disclosure. It is a factor of inherent risk, control risk and detection risk.

Inherent risk: The susceptibility of a transaction, account balance or disclosure to a misstatement that could be material, either individually or when aggregated with other misstatements, before consideration of any related controls. Examples of inherent risk factors include complexity, subjectivity, change, uncertainty and the risk of management bias or fraud.

Control risk: The risk that a misstatement that could occur in a transaction, account balance or disclosure and that could be material, either individually or when aggregated with other misstatements, will not be prevented, or detected and corrected, by the entity's internal control. Auditors therefore need to understand the controls in place within an entity as a way of addressing inherent risk.

2.1 The audit risk model

The model works by **isolating** elements of the audit process and reviewing each one to see what the impact on audit work will be. The various elements are as follows:

Inherent risk

Such risk is always present in areas of the **client** that are **susceptible** or prone to fraud or error (these are then prioritised on a **spectrum of inherent risk** by impact and likelihood)

Audit risk = Inherent risk × Control risk × Detection risk

Audit risk

This is the risk that you give an **incorrect opinion** – for example, the auditor may wish to limit the chance of this happening to only **5%** (ie working towards **95% accuracy**)

Control risk

This is another risk only ever present at **clients**, representing the risk of controls not preventing or detecting fraud or error (eg human error or management override)

Note. Together, inherent risk and control risk make up the risk of material misstatement.

Where does **detection risk** come into the formula then?

KEY TERM

Detection risk: Detection risk is the risk that audit procedures will not detect a misstatement. It is a representation of the acceptable amount of risk faced by the auditor. As inherent and control risk increase, the level of acceptable detection risk decreases and the auditor therefore performs more testing to keep audit risk at an acceptable level.

During the process of testing to address detection risk, **sampling** (which we will cover in more detail in a later chapter) will be used frequently – however, this exposes the auditor to two types of detection risk that you need to know about – **sampling risk** and **non-sampling risk**.

KEY TERM

Sampling risk: The risk that occurs every time a sample is selected and represents the risk that the sample does not adequately represent the population.

Non-sampling risk: Subtly different from sampling risk and occurs from poor interpretation of a sample by the auditor. For example, the auditor may have limited experience of sampling and may have selected a suitable sample but fails to derive the right conclusions from the data obtained (this may occur if the auditor is short of time or does not fully understand the client).

In general terms, the audit risk model could be looked at as a **mathematical equation** where you are looking for the **balancing figure**. Detection risk does just that by considering the **desired audit risk** and the likely **inherent** and **control risks** posed by the client – the auditor then has to consider the amount of work that needs to be done to balance the equation.

(FRC, 2024a)

Activity 1: Audit risk (1)

Audit risk consists of inherent risk, control risk and detection risk, which is made up of sampling and non-sampling risk.

Required

For each of the following, identify the type of risk that is being described.

Description	Risk
The accounting system at an audit client has just been the subject of a cyber-incident.	▼
The auditor has identified errors of £20,000 in a sample which totals £100,000 and concluded that the error rate is 80%.	▼
In response to revised audit risks, the amount of audit testing at three sites is to be increased.	▼
The auditor has decided to perform sample testing of controls within a national retailer by deciding to visit one branch.	▼
The auditor is reviewing a series of calculations that will be used to create the allowance for doubtful debts.	▼

Picklist

- Control risk
- Detection risk
- Inherent risk
- Non-sampling risk
- Sampling risk

Activity 2: Detection risk

You are the auditor of J Club Ltd and are working out how much work you need to do to stay within your 95% accuracy figure that you use in your firm's marketing literature.

Required

Using the audit risk model from above, show how much 'detective work' you will need to do in each of the following two scenarios if J Club Ltd has risks, as follows:

(1) Audit risk = 5% Inherent risk = 50% Control risk = 20%

(2) Audit risk = 5% Inherent risk = 50% Control risk = 40%

Scenario (1)	Scenario (2)
Detection risk =	Detection risk =

Activity 3: Audit risk (2)

Select whether the following statements in respect of audit risk are true or false.

Statement	True or false?
If inherent and control risk have been determined to be high, auditors will have to carry out a high level of detailed testing to render overall audit risk acceptable.	▼
The head of internal audit has just been suspended from one of your clients on suspicion of fraud. As a result, you assess that control risk has fallen.	▼
One of your largest retail clients has decided to cease taking cash at all its stores. You assess that inherent risk will fall for that client.	▼

Picklist

- False
- True

2.2 The risk assessment process

Auditors can use **graphical** means to help them assess risks by assigning each risk a category or description in terms of two characteristics:

(a) **Likelihood** – how possible a risk is to occur

(b) **Impact** – if it does occur, how significant will it be

Risks can then be plotted on a **risk matrix** like this:

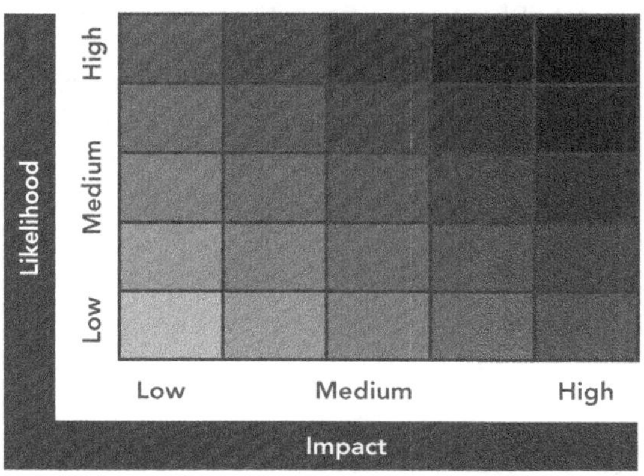

The higher the assessment of risk, the closer to the top right-hand corner it will appear and thus the risk will be assessed as being more significant.

As an alternative to a graphical representation of risk assessment, a **numerical grade** may be assigned using a similar approach to the **fraud matrix** we covered in Chapter 1. Impact and likelihood are both scored for each risk being assessed (for example, from 1 to 5) and then these scores are multiplied to give a product (in this case, anything from 1 to 25). The higher the numerical grade, the higher the risk.

Clearly, any form of assessment will be subjective to some extent, so the auditor's **professional judgement** will be important here.

2.3 Conditions necessary to demonstrate professional scepticism

In its 2012 publication on professional scepticism, the **FRC** identified **conditions** that it felt were **necessary for auditors** to be able to **demonstrate** the **appropriate** degree of **professional scepticism.** As we are currently considering the assessment of audit risk, it now seems appropriate for us to consider some of the **behavioural** and **organisational factors** that **support** an **appropriately sceptical audit**. The required conditions can be applied to various groups involved in the audit and are summarised in the following table.

Groups	Conditions
Individual auditors	Need to be professionally curious, sufficiently informed about the client and possess the confidence to challenge evidence if required.
Engagement teams	Share knowledge about the client, making appropriate decisions and revisions about the audit that evolve as evidence is collected.
Audit firms	Foster a culture of scepticism and a rigorous system of quality via appropriate recruitment, training, supervision, review, coaching and consultation. Within the firm, both teams and individual auditors are to be supported in demonstrating scepticism especially when there is potential evidence of fraud or error due to directors' actions or motivations.
Audit committees and management	The audit committee has an important role to play in supporting the external audit process by dealing constructively with any challenge made by the auditor as part of its role in displaying suitable levels of professional scepticism.

3 Analytical procedures and audit risk

Much of the evidence gathering that the auditor does is based on the verification techniques that we will meet later in the course. However, we can consider the **first** of these – **analytical procedures** – which is based on the auditor's ability to **interpret financial information**.

At the **risk assessment stage** of the audit, **risk assessment procedures** help to identify aspects of the entity being audited that the auditor might not have been aware of, using analytical procedures to identify **plausible relationships** between items of **financial** and **non-financial information** (FRC, 2025b). Broadly speaking, **assets** should not be **overstated** nor **liabilities understated** when supported by relevant data (such as revenues or purchases). Examples of the **type of relationships** sought could include:

- Consistent amounts of non-current assets, working capital and expenditure for a specific level of activity (eg consistent receivables and revenues increases)
- Consistent lengths of time taken to collect debts or pay invoices
- Consistent amounts of return for a given amount of investment in non-current assets
- Consistent amounts of debt to equity

The amount of consistency in all these areas is assessed over **a number of time frames** to allow the auditor to **pinpoint** any **specific areas of risk**. There are a number of important accounting ratios that could be used for this:

Return on capital employed (ROCE)	Operating profit / Capital employed × 100 (Where Capital employed = total equity + non-current liabilities)
Return on shareholders' funds	Profit after tax / Total equity × 100
Gross profit margin*	Gross profit / Revenue × 100
Operating profit margin*	Operating profit / Revenue × 100
*These two margins should be calculated in total and by product, area and month/quarter if possible.	
Expense/revenue percentage	Specified expense / Revenue × 100
Current ratio	Current assets / Current liabilities (Answer equals X:1)
Quick ratio or 'acid test' ratio	(Current assets – inventories) / Current liabilities (Answer equals X:1)
Inventory turnover	Cost of sales / Inventories (Answer equals X times)
Inventory holding period(days)	Inventories / Cost of sales × 365
Trade receivables collection period (days)	Trade receivables / Revenue × 365
Trade payables payment period (days)	Trade payables / Cost of sales × 365
Working capital cycle (days)	Inventory holding period (days) + trade receivables collection period (days) – trade payables payment period (days)
Asset turnover (net assets)	Revenue / (Total assets – current liabilities) (Answer equals X times)
Asset turnover (non-current assets)	Revenue / Non-current assets (Answer equals X times)
Interest cover	Operating profit / Finance costs (ie, interest) (Answer equals X times)
Gearing	Total debt / (Total debt + total equity) × 100 (Where total debt is all non-current liabilities only)

You should be familiar with these ratios from your other studies. Remember that ratios mean very little when used in isolation. They should be **calculated for previous periods** and for **comparable companies**. Audit working papers should contain summarised accounts and the chosen ratios for prior years. In addition to looking at the more usual ratios, the auditors should consider examining **other ratios** that may be **relevant** to the particular **client's business**, such as revenue per passenger mile for an airline operator client, or fees per partner for a professional office.

One further important technique is to examine **important related accounts** in conjunction with each other. It is often the case that revenue and expense accounts are related to statement of financial position accounts and comparisons should be made to ensure that the relationships are reasonable.

Activity 4: IZK Ltd

Statement of financial position as at 30 September 20X6

	20X6 £	20X5 £
ASSETS		
Non-current assets		
Property, plant and equipment	46,595	41,675
Current assets		
Inventories	60,120	58,675
Trade and other receivables	140,674	124,968
Cash and cash equivalents	17,547	6,617
	218,341	190,260
Total assets	264,936	231,935
EQUITY AND LIABILITIES		
Equity		
Share capital	1,000	1,000
Retained earnings	184,187	142,039
	185,187	143,039
Non-current liabilities		
Bank loans	4,762	14,910
Current liabilities		
Trade and other payables	74,987	73,986
Total liabilities	79,749	88,896
Total equity and liabilities	264,936	231,935

Required

Use analytical procedures to determine FOUR balances from IZK Ltd that you would investigate further for risk of material misstatement – select your answers from the list below:

- **Bank loans**
- **Cash and cash equivalents**
- **Property, plant and equipment**
- **Retained earnings**
- **Share capital**
- **Trade and other payables**
- **Trade and other receivables**

Activity 5: Bucket Ltd

The external auditor is required to undertake analytical procedures as part of the planning process in order to identify and evaluate the risks of material misstatement of figures in the financial statements. The results of the analytical procedures conducted on trade receivables and trade payables in the financial statements of an audit client are shown below.

Required

Select whether the results indicate that trade receivables and trade payables at Bucket Ltd may have been understated or overstated.

The results show that, compared with the previous year:

Results	Impact?
Trade receivables has increased by 25% and revenue has increased by 7%	▼
Trade payables has decreased by 5% and purchases has increased by 4%	▼

Picklist

- Overstated
- Understated

4 Materiality

KEY TERM

Materiality: If either the omission or misstatement of an item could reasonably affect the economic decisions of users of a set of financial statements, then that item is considered material to those financial statements.

We have already met the term **material misstatement** when discussing the auditor's objectives, and it is also relevant when evaluating **audit risk**.

Materiality is important as it **determines** the threshold above which **further audit work** becomes necessary, as well as confirming those **misstatements** or **omissions** that will have to be **considered as part of the audit opinion**.

4.1 Evaluation of materiality

The auditor must calculate a suitable level of materiality for the financial statements as a whole. This will be expressed in **quantitative terms**, often as a percentage of a significant benchmark in the financial statements.

Calculating materiality will always be a matter of **professional judgement**, so these percentages will not simply be applied without thought, but a useful guide to materiality levels is to consider that something is material if it is:

- 5–10% of profit before tax
- 1–2% of revenue
- 2–5% of total assets

The **more risky** an audit is perceived to be, the **lower the materiality level** gets, so **more things are tested**.

The auditor may need to calculate materiality levels for **specific items** in financial statements which are particularly significant to users for any reason. Some items might be material simply because of what they are, such as **revenue recognition**, which is always considered to have a higher degree of risk.

Other matters may be considered material in **qualitative terms** – for example, due to the legal restrictions around directors' remuneration disclosures in the UK, any matter relating to directors in financial statements is likely to be considered **material by nature**.

In addition, a misstatement might be considered material because of its **effect**. For example, if a small misstatement made the company breach a covenant made with its bank, it might be considered material.

Activity 6: Material or not?

Profit is £100,000 and materiality has been set at 5% of profit.

Required

Select whether the following items are likely to be considered material or not material.

Item	Material?
There is an error in receivables, value £7,500.	▼
A loan to a director has been disclosed in the financial statement at £2,000. Actually, the correct sum is £2,010.	▼
The company is required to keep a current asset ratio of 2:1. An error of £100 has been found in receivables, which will cause the ratio to drop below this level.	▼

Picklist

- Material
- Not material

4.2 Performance materiality

KEY TERM

Performance materiality: The amount or amounts set by the auditor at less than materiality for the financial statements as a whole. This reduces to an appropriately low level the probability that the aggregate of uncorrected and undetected misstatements exceeds materiality for the financial statements as a whole.

Auditors set **performance materiality** as part of risk assessment and **to decide on further audit work**.

Setting one level of materiality means that there could be items **below** this level which are misstated but not classed as material and hence not tested – if there were **several** of these and they contained some form of **misstatement**, there is a risk that, **in aggregate**, they could constitute a **material misstatement** that the auditor never knew about.

To address this risk, a **second** level of materiality is set by the auditor and used to select specific amounts where the risk of **aggregate immaterial misstatements** is highest. It is again a matter of **professional judgement** for the auditor on both the **amount** and the **classes of transaction or account balance selected**. This is called **performance materiality**. You will explore this idea further when considering the conclusion of the audit and how to communicate your findings.

4.3 Revision of materiality as the audit progresses

The auditor shall **revise materiality** for the financial statements as a whole (and, if applicable, the materiality level or levels for particular classes of transactions, account balances or disclosures) in the event of **becoming aware of information during the audit** that would have caused the auditor to have determined a **different amount (or amounts) initially**.

If the auditor concludes that a **lower materiality** for the financial statements as a whole (and, if applicable, materiality level or levels for particular classes of transactions, account balances or disclosures) **than that initially determined is appropriate**, the auditor shall determine whether it is necessary to **revise performance materiality**, and whether the **nature, timing and extent of the further audit procedures remain appropriate.**

(FRC, 2025c)

4.4 'Material' or 'material and pervasive'?

You may be asked to differentiate between the terms 'material' and 'material and pervasive' when evaluating the materiality of a misstatement or similar issue. The term **'material and pervasive'** is defined in auditing standards as follows:

KEY TERM

Material and pervasive:

- Are not confined to specific elements, accounts or items of the financial statements
- If so confined, represent or could represent a substantial proportion of the financial statements
- In relation to disclosures, are fundamental to users' understanding of the financial statements

(FRC, 2025d)

Activity 7: Materiality issues

Select whether the following statements in respect of materiality are true or false.

Statement	True or false?
Performance materiality should be set at more than materiality for the financial statements as a whole.	▼
Materiality is a measure of the importance of items to a reader of financial statements.	▼
Items may be material due to their size, nature or effect on the financial statements.	▼
A building carried in the financial statements is judged to be 'material and pervasive' if it represents 70% of total assets and 150% of profit before tax and is subject to an impairment review due to extensive damage. It is the only premises of a trading company that cannot relocate due to commercial pressure.	▼

Picklist

- False
- True

Chapter summary

- Auditors start to evaluate the planning process by attempting to understand the entity that is being audited, both at the financial statement level (risks that affect the whole financial statements) and at the assertion level (more specific issues related to the way that certain amounts are carried within the financial statements).
- Risk assessment procedures require an understanding of the factors that go into creating audit risk:
  - Inherent risk – the susceptibility of certain things being misstated (this is client-driven).
  - Control risk – the inability of systems of internal control to deal with such inherent risks (this is also client-driven).
  - Detection risk – the risk that the auditor does not do enough testing to take account of inherent and control risk. This is auditor-driven and includes sampling risk (the risk that a sample is not representative of the population) and non-sampling risk (the risk that results of testing are misinterpreted).
- Risk can be assessed and expressed both graphically on a risk matrix and numerically by awarding a suitable grade
- Analytical procedures are used to identify and understand risks within a set of financial statements and use techniques such as ratios, comparisons and other techniques to understand profitability, operating and gearing issues presented by an audited entity.
- Materiality is the term used to describe the significance of certain items within the financial statements depending on the importance placed upon them by users of those financial statements. It can be assessed numerically (such as a percentage of profit before tax or total assets) but also qualitatively (by nature, such as a related party transaction). Items can be assessed as not just 'material' but also 'material and pervasive' if they meet certain criteria relating to their size and impact which auditors also need to consider.
- Performance materiality is an amount set at below materiality to allow the auditor to test for items where, in the auditor's judgement, there may be misstatements that are individually immaterial but in aggregate, they could represent a material misstatement.
- Materiality is one of the single most difficult areas for the auditor due to the heavy reliance on judgement to make it work effectively.

Activity answers

Activity 1: Audit risk (1)

Description	Risk
The accounting system at an audit client has just been the subject of a cyber-incident.	Control risk
The auditor has identified errors of £20,000 in a sample which totals £100,000 and concluded that the error rate is 80%.	Non-sampling risk
In response to revised audit risks, the amount of audit testing at three sites is to be increased.	Detection risk
The auditor has decided to perform sample testing of controls within a national retailer by deciding to visit one branch.	Sampling risk
The auditor is reviewing a series of calculations that will be used to create the allowance for doubtful debts.	Inherent risk

Although a cyber-incident might introduce inherent risks, there is a risk that the accounting system (which is part of the entity's system of internal control and critical to the preparation of the financial statements) has been affected, meaning that control risk is increased.

The auditor has calculated the rate of correct items, not the error rate (it should be 20% not 80%) meaning that non-sampling risk arises.

Increasing the extent of audit testing in response to changes in audit risk is an illustration of how detection risk responds to factors within the audit.

Although the one branch may be significant, it seems unlikely that the sample is representative of the population, meaning that sampling risk has arisen.

Calculations for doubtful debts are likely to be complex and subject to both change and uncertainty, making them inherently risky.

Activity 2: Detection risk

(1) $5\% = 50\% \times 20\% \times 50\%$

(2) $5\% = 50\% \times 40\% \times 25\%$

Detection risk is the risk that audit procedures do not detect a misstatement – it is logical that, in order to reduce this risk to a figure as close to zero as possible, the auditor must perform relatively more work; hence, reducing the risks of not detecting a misstatement, whether caused by fraud or error.

In the examples above, the second scenario shows a company where controls are twice as risky (or half as good) and, as such, we cannot rely on J Club's controls in scenario (ii) as much we did in scenario (i). In order to keep the risk of our firm giving an incorrect opinion to 5% with fewer controls to rely on, we therefore have to screen more transactions ourselves under scenario (ii) in the absence of J Club's own controls (in other words, as detection risk falls, the amount of work done by the auditor needs to increase to maintain the same level of audit risk overall).

Had J Club's inherent risks changed, this would have affected our detection risk as well, in line with the equation, and potentially given us a different balancing figure.

Activity 3: Audit risk (2)

Statement	True or false?
If inherent and control risk have been determined to be high, auditors will have to carry out a high level of detailed testing to render overall audit risk acceptable.	True
The head of internal audit has just been suspended from one of your clients on suspicion of fraud. As a result, you assess that control risk has fallen.	False
One of your largest retail clients has decided to cease taking cash at all its stores. You assess that inherent risk will fall for that client.	True

If inherent and control risk are high, detection risk will need to be low, which means a high level of testing must be carried out.

Being unable to trust the work of the internal auditor means that controls are less likely to be relied upon and as such control risk rises.

Cash is an inherently risky item due to its portability and anonymity, so reducing the reliance on this as part of the client's business will mean the inherent risk of the audit falls.

Activity 4: IZK Ltd

The four balances most likely to need review from the statement of financial position would be **property, plant and equipment, trade and other receivables, cash and cash equivalents** and **bank loans**. Non-current assets are usually depreciated, so we would expect to see a fall in their value but in 20X6 they have increased – this is not unusual, but begs the question of how they could have increased when:

(1) No revaluation reserve exists

(2) No fresh share capital has been issued

(3) Bank loans have fallen, suggesting that no new debt has been taken out (we may have seen a repayment of some debt, but see the next point)

(4) Cash has risen, suggesting that cash balances were not used to redeem the bank loan. So how did the company afford new property, plant and equipment?

There are enough questions here to cause the auditor to be alerted to the risk of material misstatement in the statement of financial position – further audit procedures will then be prompted as a result of this basic analysis.

Activity 5: Bucket Ltd

Results	Impact?
Trade receivables has increased by 25% and revenue has increased by 7%	Overstated
Trade payables has decreased by 5% and purchases has increased by 4%	Understated

Activity 6: Material or not?

Item	Material?
There is an error in receivables, value £7,500.	Material
A loan to a director has been disclosed in the financial statement at £2,000. Actually, the correct sum is £2,010.	Material
The company is required to keep a current asset ratio of 2:1. An error of £100 has been found in receivables, which will cause the ratio to drop below this level.	Material

Materiality will be set at £5,000 (5% × £100,000) making £7,500 a material balance.

Although the loan is below the materiality threshold, the fact that is to a director (a related party) means that it is likely to be material.

Again, although £100 is below the materiality threshold, it has a material impact due to the covenant described.

Activity 7: Materiality issues

Statement	True or false?
Performance materiality should be set at more than materiality for the financial statements as a whole.	True
Materiality is a measure of the importance of items to a reader of financial statements.	True
Items may be material due to their size, nature or effect on the financial statements.	True
A building carried in the financial statements is judged to be 'material and pervasive' if it represents 70% of total assets and 150% of profit before tax and is subject to an impairment review due to extensive damage. It is the only premises of a trading company that cannot relocate due to commercial pressure.	True

Performance materiality should be set at **less** than materiality for the financial statements as a whole.

Tutorial note. Determining whether something is 'material and pervasive' is usually going to require a degree of judgement by the auditor. However, in this case, it is probably more clear-cut as, although this relates to only one item, it represents a substantial proportion of the financial statements, and the impairment is likely to substantially affect the future of the company.

Test your learning

1 **Select which ONE of the following statements best summarises why auditors must gain an understanding of the entity using the appropriate tick box.**

	✓
In order to understand internal control systems	
In order to be able to assess risks	
In order to see what items there are to be audited	
In order to eliminate items from testing	

2 **Complete the definitions using the items in the picklist below.**

[▼] risk is the risk that the auditors give an [▼] opinion on the financial statements.

[▼] risk is the risk that the entity's internal control system will not prevent or detect and correct errors.

[▼] risk is the risk that items will be misstated due to their [▼] or due to their [▼].

[▼] risk is the risk that misstatements will exist in financial statements and the auditors will not discover them.

Picklist

- Audit
- Context
- Control
- Detection
- Inappropriate
- Incorrect
- Inherent
- Nature

3 **Select whether the following statements concerning audit risks are true or false.**

Statement	True or false?
Auditors cannot affect inherent and control risk as inherent and control risks are the risks that errors will arise in the financial statements as a result of control problems or the nature of items in the financial statements of the entity. The auditors cannot control those factors.	▼

Statement	True or false?
If inherent and control risk are high, detection risk should be rendered low to come to an overall acceptable level of risk. In order for detection risk to be low, the auditors will have to carry out a low level of testing.	▼

Picklist

- False
- True

4 When planning an audit of financial statements, the auditor is required to consider how factors such as the entity's operating environment and its system of control affect the risk of material misstatement in the financial statements.

Required

Select whether the following factors are likely to increase or reduce the risk of misstatement.

Factor	Impact?
The control environment is weak and there is considerable pressure on management to improve results year on year.	▼
Management has implemented improvements in controls as a result of weaknesses identified last year.	▼

Picklist

- Increase
- Reduce

5 **Select whether the following statements in respect of materiality are true or false.**

Statement	True or false?
Materiality is the concept of significance to users of the financial statements.	▼
'Material and pervasive' in relation to disclosures means anything related to directors.	▼

Picklist

- False
- True

6 When planning an audit of financial statements, the auditor is required to consider how factors such as the entity's nature and operating environment affect the risk of material misstatement in the financial statements.

Required

Select whether the following factors are likely to increase or reduce the risk of misstatement.

The company has diversified its operations during the year.	▼
The company has discontinued operations in its riskiest operating area during the year.	▼

Picklist

- Increase
- Reduce

4 Evidence and the audit approach

Learning outcomes

Having studied this chapter, you will be able to:

4	**Evaluate internal control systems as part of the audit process**
4.1	**Internal controls and their impact on the audit approach** Learners need to understand: 4.1.1 why auditors need to understand the company's internal controls 4.1.2 the differences between tests of controls and substantive procedures. Learners need to be able to: 4.1.3 determine when to use a mixture of tests of controls and substantive procedures or substantive procedures only 4.1.4 identify how errors and irregularities can be mitigated by control procedures 4.1.5 identify suitable tests of control for accounting systems.
5	**Understand procedures for obtaining sufficient and appropriate evidence**
5.1	**Audit assertions and audit procedures** Learners need to understand: 5.1.1 assertions about transactions: • occurrence • completeness • accuracy • cut off • classification • presentation 5.1.2 assertions about balances: • existence • rights and obligations • completeness • accuracy, valuation and allocation • classification • presentation.

5.2	**Sampling techniques** Learners need to understand: 5.2.1 statistical and non-statistical sampling methods 5.2.2 the advantages and disadvantages of different sampling methods: • stratification • value-weighted selection • random selection • systematic selection • monetary unit sampling • haphazard selection • block selection. Learners need to be able to: 5.2.3 distinguish between sampling methods and when they should be used 5.2.4 identify factors affecting sample sizes.
5.3	**Methods used to obtain audit evidence** Learners need to understand: 5.3.1 types of verification techniques: • inspection • observation • external confirmation • recalculation • reperformance • analytical procedures • enquiry 5.3.2 the reliability and relevance of different sources of audit evidence. Learners need to be able to: 5.3.3 identify when it is appropriate to use each type of verification technique.
5.4	**Use of digital techniques in auditing** Learners need to understand: 5.4.1 types of digital techniques: • test data • integrated test facilities • audit software • data analytic tools 5.4.2 how digital techniques are used to test controls and interrogate the organisation's files 5.4.3 the benefits and drawbacks of: • digital techniques • remote auditing.

Assessment context

Tasks 7 and 8 in the assessment will be supported by this topic as we look at how to obtain audit procedures, evidence and sampling using a variety of question types.

Qualification context

There are some new pieces of terminology introduced here – evidence, sampling and digital techniques in auditing – but although they are all new, they exist in areas that you have seen elsewhere in your AAT studies (such as final accounts and accounting software).

Business context

Evidence is the oxygen without which the auditor cannot breathe: the more of it there is, the more likely it is that the auditor is able to achieve their overall objective – providing an audit opinion. In the real world, the collection of evidence is the most time-consuming part of any audit.

Chapter overview

Evidence and the audit approach

- **Methods for collecting audit evidence**
  - Verification techniques
  - Tests of control
  - Substantive testing
  - Substantive analytical procedures
  - Identifying the most appropriate mixture of tests to use
- **Sufficient appropriate audit evidence**
  - Reliable evidence
  - Relevant evidence – the use of assertions
  - Direction of testing
- **Digital techniques in auditing**
  - Audit software
  - Using the client's own system
  - Data analytic tools
  - Remote auditing
- **Sampling techniques**
  - Non-statistical sampling
  - Stratification
  - How to pick the sample
  - Confidence level
  - Advantages and disadvantages of different sampling methods

Introduction

We are now in a position to start collecting the evidence we need to be able to form our opinion on the financial statements. Within this chapter, you will learn about the various techniques that exist for collecting evidence and when they should be used. You will also learn about what it means to generate 'sufficient' and 'appropriate' audit evidence and what that will require in terms of suitable audit procedures.

You will then learn about the various techniques that exist for the auditor to collect this evidence. As well as considering the emerging role that technology plays, we will consider the use of samples to derive conclusions about the population.

1 Methods for collecting audit evidence

In order to reach a valid opinion, you need **enough** of the **right kind** of evidence – we will consider how we determine whether we have this later, but first, let's look at the various techniques that exist in order to **collect evidence**.

1.1 Verification techniques

Auditors perform tests to obtain evidence throughout the audit, and such testing usually requires a number of **verification techniques (AEEIOUR)**:

- **A**nalytical procedures (introduced in a previous chapter and covered in more detail below)
- **E**nquiry (asking questions and confirming facts to obtain evidence) and **E**xternal confirmation (with third parties for values or conditions)
- **I**nspection (of records or other documents – sometimes called 'vouching' – as well as physical inspection of tangible assets)
- **O**bservation (of staff performing various activities)
- Recalc**U**lation (of items and amounts) or **R**e-performance (of activities and procedures) which is used to evaluate how a control is applied in practice.

KEY TERM

Analytical procedures: Evaluations of financial information made by a study of financial and non-financial data.

Analytical procedures comprise the following activities:

- **Comparison** of actual with budget, across different business units or even with similar firms and industry averages. This could work for absolute amounts, percentages like profit margin or even indicators such as receivables days and should be performed across a variety of time frames.
- **Calculation** of ratios (such as net and gross margins) and **explanations** to support them (eg a 10% increase in expenditure coming from 10% more sales activity).
- **Credibility checks**, such as looking at a year's revenue for a manufacturer and dividing it by the number of working days to get a 'feel' for the implied level of daily activity, and **proof in total** (such as the relationship of payroll costs to the number of employees and their likely average pay).

A variety of methods can be used to perform these procedures, ranging from **simple comparisons** to **complex analysis** using statistics, on a company level, branch level or individual account level. The choice of procedures is a matter for the auditors' professional judgement.

Auditors are required to use analytical procedures as part of the risk assessment process at the **planning** stage of the audit, to:

- Identify risk areas
- Determine the nature, timing and extent of procedures

The auditor may also use analytical procedures as **substantive procedures** (we will define these later in this chapter).

There are a number of factors which the auditors should consider when deciding whether to use analytical procedures as substantive procedures, such as:

- Whether the procedures are **suitable** to obtain evidence about the relevant **assertions** (given the assessed risk for those assertions, which we will also define later in this chapter)
- Whether the data the auditor is using is reliable, available and relevant

When analytical procedures identify **significant fluctuations or unexpected relationships**, the auditors must investigate by obtaining adequate explanations from management and appropriate corroborative evidence. Investigations will start with enquiries to management and then **confirmation** of management's responses.

All these verification techniques can be used in a variety of different circumstances: first, let's think about systems of internal controls and how we might test them.

1.2 Tests of control

KEY TERM

Tests of control: Tests to obtain evidence about the effective operation of the accounting and internal control systems.

We learned in the first chapter that an organisation relies on its system of internal control for a variety of reasons. Auditors are most interested in the system of internal control that supports the **quality** of external reporting when producing the financial statements to assess the **risk of material misstatement** within the financial statements and to **comply with auditing standards** and **plan the audit effectively** (although that is underpinned by the importance of preventing and detecting **fraud**, compliance with **laws and regulations** and **safeguarding assets**). In general, with the exception of analytical procedures and external confirmations, the verification techniques described above (EIOUR) can all be used by auditors to test the controls in place within an organisation.

Illustration 1: Tests of control

Consider the following examples of tests of control that could be found in a purchases system:

Audit test and description:	Working paper:	Performed by:
(a) Select a sample of 10 invoices from the Purchase Invoice Listing (PIL) and: - Inspect the invoice for evidence of matching to goods received note (GRN) and authorisation - Re-perform matching of invoice to GRN		
(b) For a sample of 15 PIL totals: - Recalculate to batch header slip ensuring the slip is initialled - Inspect batch book to ensure that all batches have been processed and that any outstanding batches have been followed up		
(c) Observe and enquire into the procedures for preparing suppliers' statement reconciliations		

Audit test and description:	Working paper:	Performed by:
(d) Select a sample of 10 invoices from the PIL and: - Ensure casts and extensions have been checked - Re-perform casts and extensions		
(e) Select a sample of suppliers' statement reconciliations (one month in detail; review others) and re-perform these reconciliations, ensuring those statements not in agreement have been followed up		
(f) Inspect one month's purchase ledger control account reconciliation in detail and review for other months		
(g) Review the file of unmatched GRNs and enquire into old items still outstanding		

Activity 1: Controls and tests – purchases

Accounting systems information – purchases

A company, Glad Rags Ltd, keeps basic stocks of all the fabric and threads required to manufacture goods from their catalogue. When stocks fall to a certain level, the stores manager requisitions a pre-set amount of that stock. There are certain fabrics that are only used for a limited number of stocks. That fabric will only be reordered if a sales order is placed for items requiring the fabric.

When the purchases department receives a requisition, they place the order with the approved supplier at a pre-arranged price. An order document is written out and kept in the orders pending file.

When the fabric or thread is received, the stores manager ensures that the quality is suitable and checks the goods against the order. The order is then passed to the accounts department and placed in the pending invoices file.

When the invoice is received, the accounts assistant, Beth Simpkins, checks the invoices against the order to ensure the price and quantity are correct and checks the VAT has been calculated correctly. She initials the invoices to show that these checks have been carried out and gives the invoice a sequence number. The invoice is then entered into the purchase ledger on the computer.

Beth prepares cheques for payment at the end of each fortnight and passes them to the director, Gladys Barton, for signature and approval. The invoices are included with the cheques as evidence of the money owed.

Most suppliers send statements at the end of the month, which Beth reconciles to the purchase ledger balances. The purchase ledger control account is agreed to the total of the purchase ledger balances at the end of the month.

Required

Using the accounting system for purchases described for Glad Rags Ltd, identify FIVE controls and suggest tests of control that could be performed to confirm the application of each control.

Lay out your answer in a table using controls in the left-hand column and tests of control in the right-hand column.

Activity 2: Controls and tests – payroll

Accounting systems information – payroll

There are two payrolls at Glad Rags Ltd, which are computerised and prepared by the director, Gladys Barton. Machining staff are paid by piece, which is recorded and approved by the factory overseer, Peter Benning. Machining staff are paid weekly. Office and other administrative staff are paid a standard salary on a monthly basis.

The weekly payroll produces an exception report if machining staff are paid in excess of 20% more than their weekly average over the year. This exception report is checked back to the piece sheets which are prepared and approved by Peter Benning. Machinists are paid in cash which must be collected personally and signed for by the employee.

Monthly payments are made by automatic bank transfer from Glad Rags' bank account to the employees' bank account.

Required

Using the accounting system for payroll described for Glad Rags Ltd, identify FOUR controls and suggest tests of control that could be performed to confirm the application of each control.

Lay out your answer in a table using controls in the left-hand column and tests of control in the right-hand column.

1.3 Substantive testing

KEY TERM

> **Substantive testing:** Audit procedures designed to detect material misstatements in the financial statements at the assertion level. They comprise of tests of detail and substantive analytical procedures.
>
> **Tests of detail:** Audit procedures that test classes of transaction, account balances and disclosures, usually through detailed inspection of invoices, documents and assets.

When performing **tests of control**, if we **trust** the **controls in place within a system**, we can test them and the results of this testing will provide us with some **assurance** that the **output** of such systems can be used to produce the entity's financial statements.

Testing controls alone, however, is **not enough** to form an opinion, due to the various **limitations** of internal controls that we saw earlier. Consequently, we need to make sure that the **actual balances and amounts** themselves, which have been included in the financial statements, can be trusted (rather than the processes used to generate them). This is referred to as **substantive testing** and will **always be carried out to some extent** during an audit.

- Even if we **trusted the controls** in place, we would still use an amount of substantive testing to **supplement** this, with the extent dependent on the outcome of tests of control.

- If we could place **little or no assurance on controls** (or, in the case of a smaller entity, controls were not cost-effective) the level of substantive testing would be **increased**.

You have already seen the sort of procedures that auditors make use of when performing **both tests of control** and **substantive testing (AEEIOUR)** but they are sometimes **difficult** to tell apart and could form part of a question in your assessment.

Activity 3: Controls or substantive?

Are each of the following audit tests a test of control or a substantive test?

Audit test	Test of control or substantive test?
Selection of ten invoices to test for correct authorisation in line with official signatory list	▼
Tracing ten non-current assets back to initial purchases invoices to verify their value	▼
Tracing ten non-current assets back to initial purchases invoices to verify they have been allocated to the correct cost centre by the accounts clerk	▼

Picklist

- Substantive test
- Test of control

1.4 Substantive analytical procedures

We saw the use of analytical procedures earlier; however, auditing standards also allow the use of substantive analytical procedures – what are they?

Activity 4: Ginger Ltd

Ginger Ltd is a hotel chain with 10 hotels. Each hotel has 100 rooms and achieves around 55% occupancy throughout the year. The average room rate is £75 inclusive of all charges. You are the audit senior and have the draft financial statements for the year just ended.

The audit junior has been tasked with carrying out substantive analytical procedures to verify the annual revenue figure for Ginger of £15 million but is unsure whether or not he needs any other information.

Required

(a) Is any further information required for us to verify this balance using substantive analytical procedures? Select the most appropriate option from the picklist below.

[▼]

Picklist

- Bar and restaurant spend per customer
- Length of stay per customer
- No further information required
- Number of nights open during the year

(b) **Assume that the average room rate for Ginger Ltd is now £50 but the rest of the data is the same. Prepare extracts for reporting these findings to the audit manager, along with the implications of these findings for the audit plan.**

1.5 Identifying the most appropriate mixture of tests to use

In your assessment, you are likely to be asked to determine the most appropriate mixture of tests of control and substantive testing and justify your selection. To help you with this, let's consider the following activity.

Activity 5: Mixed audit approach or substantive procedures only?

For each of the following scenarios, identify the most suitable audit approach.

Scenario	Approach
Scoot Ltd is a new company that has not been audited before and is dominated by its managing director and his informal operating style. Sales are of greatest importance to him as the company attempts to break into a competitive retail sector.	▼
Whitney plc is an established listed company that operates in a stable market with strong governance procedures, including an audit committee.	▼
The board of Marine Ltd has just informed its external auditor that it wishes to replace its ledger systems due to a number of errors identified in its management accounts.	▼

Picklist

- Substantive procedures only, with no tests of control
- Tests of control and substantive procedures

2 Sufficient appropriate audit evidence

Previously, we stated that the auditor is required to obtain sufficient, appropriate audit evidence in order to support their opinion that the financial statements are free from material misstatement. What do these terms mean?

Audit evidence

- **Sufficiency** *('enough of')*
  'Sufficiency' is **subjective** and based on the auditor's **professional judgement**.
  Results of **systems testing** and **assessments** of **risk** and **materiality** are used.
  Additional procedures can be carried out if the auditor feels there is not enough evidence to form a valid conclusion.
- **Appropriateness** *('the right kind of')*
  - **Relevance**
    Relevant evidence is judged as the right kind if it helps to **prove** a **specific characteristic** that a balance or transaction should **possess** (see below).
  - **Reliability**
    Reliable evidence considers the **source** of the evidence and ensures it adds **credibility** to the overall audit process (see below).

2.1 Reliable evidence

There are some generalisations about the reliability of evidence:

- It is more reliable when it is obtained from **independent sources** outside the entity.
- If internally generated, it is more reliable if the **related controls are strong**.
- If **obtained directly by the auditor** (rather than indirectly or by inference) then it is more reliable.
- It is more reliable when in **documentary form** (such as written representations from management, rather than oral).
- It is more reliable when documents are **originals**, not photocopies or facsimiles.

2.2 Relevant evidence – the use of assertions

KEY TERM

> **Assertions:** Characteristics that all items within the financial statements (including disclosure notes) should possess in order to 'belong' there.

Consider all the **elements** of a set of financial statements – **assets**, **liabilities**, **income**, **expenditure** and all their associated **disclosures**. In order to **belong there**, each part of the financial statements has to possess some **specific characteristics** (a little like **membership requirements** for a specific club or society).

The auditor needs to make sure that if something has been included in the financial statements, **it should be there** – in order to establish this, the auditor seeks evidence that is **relevant** to confirming that the element **does possess** those characteristics required in order to belong. We refer to these characteristics as **assertions.** There are two categories of assertions:

Assertions about **classes of transactions and events and related disclosures**	**Occurrence**: transactions and events that have been recorded or disclosed have occurred and pertain to the entity. **Completeness**: all transactions and events that should have been recorded have been recorded and all related disclosures that should have been included in the financial statements have been included. **Accuracy**: amounts and other data relating to recorded transactions and events have been recorded appropriately, and related disclosures have been appropriately measured and described. **Cut-off**: transactions and events have been recorded in the correct accounting period. **Classification**: transactions and events have been recorded in the proper accounts. **Presentation**: Transactions and events are appropriately aggregated or disaggregated and are clearly described, and related disclosures are relevant and understandable in the context of the requirements of the applicable financial reporting framework.
Assertions **about account balances and related disclosures** at the period end	**Existence**: assets, liabilities, and equity interests exist. **Rights and obligations**: the entity holds or controls the rights to assets, and liabilities are the obligations of the entity. **Completeness**: all assets, liabilities and equity interests that should have been recorded have been recorded and all related disclosures that should have been included in the financial statements have been included. **Accuracy, valuation and allocation**: assets, liabilities, and equity interests are included in the financial statements at appropriate amounts and any resulting valuation or allocation adjustments are appropriately recorded and related disclosures have been appropriately measured and described. **Classification**: assets, liabilities and equity interests have been recorded in the proper accounts. **Presentation**: Assets, liabilities and equity instruments are appropriately aggregated or disaggregated and are clearly described, and related disclosures are relevant and understandable in the context of the requirements of the applicable financial reporting framework.

(FRC, 2025b)

2.3 Direction of testing

One important matter to consider is the 'direction' of a test. When devising an audit test, it's useful to think about the two types of audit evidence available:

- **Source documents** – these include **physical assets** (such as an item of inventory or a non-current asset) and documents (ie invoices, contracts, goods despatched notes, goods received notes and timesheets)

- **Financial records** – these include the financial statements and other records which are agreed to the financial statements (ie cash books, ledgers and non-current asset registers)

If auditors are testing whether something has been **understated** in the financial statements (for example, a liability such as trade payables), they must start the test at a source document and agree the source document to the financial records. If auditors are testing whether something has been **overstated** in the financial statements (for example, non-current assets or sales revenue), they start with the financial records and trace back to source documents – to ensure the item existed in the first place.

Activity 6: Assertions (1)

Consider each of the following audit tests and then select the most appropriate assertion that describes the purpose of that test.

Audit test	
Select a sample of vehicles from the list of non-current assets and obtain their certificates of ownership.	▼
Select a sample of receivables from the statement of financial position and agree to original invoices.	▼
Select a sample of receivables from the sales ledger and agree to the final amount on the statement of financial position.	▼
Trace a selection of payments included in cost of sales to original invoices.	▼

Picklist

- Completeness
- Cut-off
- Existence
- Occurrence
- Rights and obligations

Activity 7: Assertions (2)

Consider each of the following situations and select the most appropriate audit procedure for the assertion used.

Situation	Procedure
Testing cut-off for staff bonuses paid at the end of the financial year	▼
Confirming the accuracy of staff bonuses paid at the end of the financial year	▼
Confirming the value of cash investments held in a savings account by a client	▼

Picklist

- Obtaining a letter from the bank stating that a savings account is held by the client
- Obtaining a letter from the bank stating the amount of savings held by the client
- Reconciling payroll records to a schedule of staff bonus payments authorised by the finance director
- Verifying bonus payments to payroll records to determine their timing

---

Once the testing is complete and the relevant evidence has been **collected**, as with all other outputs from the audit process, it must be **recorded** and **documented** in line with ISA 230 *Audit Documentation* (paras 2 and 3).

3 Digital techniques in auditing

KEY TERM

> **Digital techniques in auditing:** Audit techniques carried out by the auditor using a computer.

Digital techniques in auditing include **simple** procedures, such as the auditor using **spreadsheets** to manipulate data, and more **complex** computer programs and techniques, such as **embedded audit facilities** which allow the auditor continuous review of the client's system. **Automated tools and techniques** can be **intrusive** and should only be used with **client permission**, as the client will not want the auditors' software to cause problems in their own computer systems.

Benefits of using digital techniques in auditing	Drawbacks of using digital techniques in auditing
This technique allows large volumes of data to be analysed at great speed, making the audit process more efficient and allowing the auditor to focus on other tasks if required.	However, like any system, they require quality data for input, otherwise the output of this process will not be reliable. Skills and experience (which may not always be available) are required to both administer and interpret the findings.

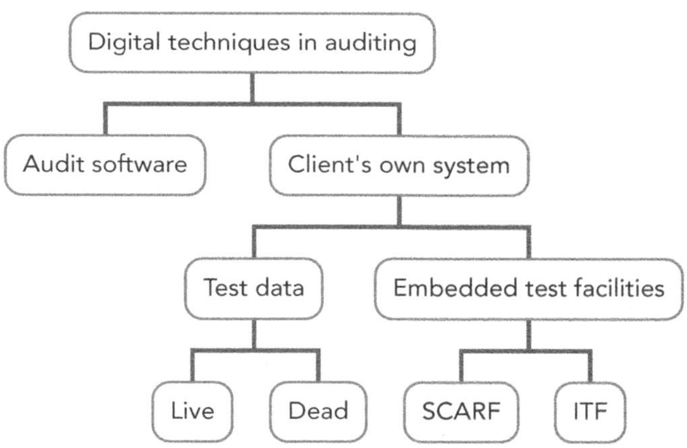

3.1 Audit software

KEY TERM

> **Audit software:** Software used by the auditor to perform testing on a client's financial systems and data.

Audit software is primarily used for **substantive testing** and is suitable for the majority of audit engagements. Data will be **downloaded from the client's system to the auditor's computer** when a number of typical tests could be performed, such as:

(a) **Reperformance of calculations** eg ageing of trade receivables, casts of day books, ledger listings or inventory reports (additional comfort is gained here as the auditor's own software is being used to generate evidence)

(b) Extraction of **samples**

(c) **Analytical review** eg ratio calculations

3.2 Using the client's own system

This is primarily used for **tests of control**, and more suited to larger audit engagements. Such testing of controls will require **significant co-operation from the client**, especially in terms of computer access time. Typical uses include:

KEY TERM

> **Test data:** The submission of 'dummy' data into the client's own system to ensure it is processed correctly, or not processed if the data is deliberately false. This can be conducted 'live' or 'dead' ie as part of normal processing or at times when the computer is not in business use.
>
> **Embedded test facilities:** These aim to extend the tests of control more fully throughout the period than test data and include use of a systems control and review file (SCARF) and integrated test facilities (ITF).
>
> **Systems Control and Review File (SCARF):** A diagnostic report of how the system is working.
>
> **Integrated Test Facilities (ITF):** A 'virtual' or 'dummy' copy of the system used for testing live data to confirm that it behaves in the way that it should.

3.3 Data analytic tools

KEY TERM

> **Data analytic tools:** The use of technology to interrogate entire data sets.

Recent advances in **big data technology** have seen automated tools and techniques evolve into something more sophisticated that could be become a real game-changer for the auditing profession. The ability to access and interrogate **entire populations of client** data using **data analytics** has meant that the auditor's scope can now be increased, allowing them to concentrate on **interpreting the messages locked inside the data** instead of spending all their time simply trying to analyse it.

Examples of the types of audit activities that could benefit from data analytics include the following:

- **Analysing data sets** for information on specific locations, products, employees or times for the purpose of identifying fraud or error
- **Reconciling activity** such as matching orders, despatch notes and invoices for evidence of misstatement
- **Inspecting journals** to identify patterns, trends and relationships that may indicate fraud

Underpinning all of this is the superior processing power that **artificial intelligence (AI)** and **machine learning** can introduce to any analysis undertaken by the auditor. Clearly, significant amounts of **training** and **investment** are required to unlock the potential of this technology, but the possibilities are almost without limit.

Activity 8: Digital techniques in auditing

For each of the procedures listed below, select the type of digital technique in auditing which would be used to perform that procedure.

Procedure	Technique
Extraction of all receivables balances older than 120 days to perform irrecoverable receivable work	▼
Input of purchases invoices with false customer numbers to ensure that the system rejects the invoices	▼
Comparison of suppliers on ledger with previous years to discover any new or missing suppliers	▼
Interrogation of a year's transactions to analyse profitability by product and store for a retailer	▼

Picklist

- Audit software
- Data analytic tools
- Integrated test facilities
- Test data

3.4 Remote auditing

As more entities make use of **integrated accounting systems** including the switch from **paper to electronic record-keeping** and **accounting software** such as Sage, Xero and QuickBooks, access to accounting information may no longer require the auditor to be on site. Although much of this technology was used beforehand, the **COVID pandemic** resulted in a number of innovative solutions to limit social interactions while still performing necessary tasks such as audits in the following ways:

- **Video-conferencing software** such as Teams or Zoom for meetings
- **Data analytics software** that can analyse accounting records transferred over secure data links
- **Document sharing software** allowed teams of auditors to operate remotely without the need to have one physical file for an audit engagement
- **Work scheduling** that is more flexible for auditors and their clients

The success of these and other technologies (such as **drones** which allow auditors to inspect assets previously unavailable to them like tall buildings or underground tunnels) since the pandemic has led to a shift in the way that audits can be conducted, many of which are designed to **save costs** and **improve efficiency** (for example, working remotely saves on the time and costs associated with travelling to audit clients).

There are inevitable **disadvantages** to remote auditing – without physically being on site, there is a risk that evidence cannot be fully validated and that the social benefit of being able to read human behaviour is absent. This will mean that greater amounts of **professional scepticism** are required and suitable levels of **professional judgement** on the most appropriate use (if any) of remote auditing.

4 Sampling techniques

According to auditing standards, the objective of the auditor, when using audit sampling, is to provide a reasonable basis for the auditor to draw conclusions about the population from which the sample is selected (FRC, 2025e).

KEY TERM

Audit sampling: Applying audit procedures to less than 100% of items within an account balance or class of transactions in such a way as to draw a conclusion on the account balance or class of transactions as a whole.

Statistical sampling: An approach to sampling that involves random selection of the sample items; and the use of probability theory to evaluate sample results including measurement of sampling risk (the risk of selecting a non-representative sample).

Sampling units: The individual items constituting a 'population' (account balance or class of transaction) – for example, a single receivable balance within total receivables or an individual sale within total revenue.

(FRC, 2025e)

The key rule of audit sampling is that all 'sampling units' must have an equal chance of being selected for testing.

As you may have gathered, sampling is closely connected with **risk** and **materiality**. Sampling affects **detection risk** because, put simply, the more items within a population that are tested, the higher the chance of the auditor finding a misstatement.

However, if the auditor does not test every single sampling unit in the population, there is a **risk** that **misstatements will not be detected**. However carefully the sample is selected, it is possible that the sample will not be representative of the population as a whole.

Sampling, therefore, **always** carries a level of detection risk. The auditor has to determine an appropriate level of this risk in order to obtain the benefit of sampling (which is that auditors don't have to test everything!). The larger the sample tested, the lower the detection risk.

4.1 Non-statistical sampling

KEY TERM

Non-statistical sampling: The use of judgement to select a sample instead of a statistical technique.

In some instances, auditors will want to exercise **judgement** and test specific items, rather than selecting a random sample.

For instance, we have already observed that auditors should test **all material items**. Therefore, if the receivables' ledger contains debts that are themselves material to the financial statements, they should be selected.

This is not a statistical sample by the above definition. As these items have been selected with bias, the auditor cannot assume that they are reflective of the rest of the population, and should not project the results of testing on these items to the rest of the population. This **more subjective** approach, where the auditor selects samples not randomly but using their professional judgement, is called non-statistical sampling.

Another example of non-statistical sampling is where the auditor believes there is a greater risk of **cut-off errors around the year-end**, and therefore focuses audit testing on the sales transactions just before, and just after, the year end.

4.2 Stratification

KEY TERM

Stratification: Dividing a population into smaller, equal-sized sub-populations, each of which is a group of sampling units, usually by value.

The **remainder** of the population should be sampled in a non-biased way. This is known as stratifying a population. Therefore, instead of testing receivables as a whole, the auditor might test two populations of receivable balances, individually material receivable balances and individually non-material receivable balances (the total of which might well be material).

In this circumstance, the auditor would not apply sampling procedures to the first population, and would instead **test all of the material balances**. The auditor would apply sampling procedures to the second population and select balances for testing. Results from the **sampled population** could be **projected** onto the rest of that sub-population to assess if total misstatements are likely to be material.

In the first population, there would be **no need to project results** because, if everything has been tested, there is nothing to project the errors against. All errors in that population should have been found.

In some audit areas, it might be more appropriate to **test 100% of items**, or a **very high percentage** of items (so that errors in the remaining balance couldn't possibly be material). An example is often additions to property, plant and equipment, where only one or two material additions may have been made in the year, and there is no need to select a sample, merely to test these items.

4.3 How to pick the sample

The important rule above comes in here. It is important that **any item in the population has a chance of being picked** – so, in general terms, the auditor should not bias the sample.

For example, if a company has two factories, one 20 miles from the auditor and the other 120 miles from the auditor, it is easier for the auditor to physically verify that the closer one exists. However, this would be putting an unreasonable bias on the sample selection.

In order to avoid bias, there are several common ways of selecting samples:

(a) By **random selection**. The auditor uses a computer program or table to (mathematically) randomly select the sample.

(b) By **systematic selection**. The auditor randomly selects the first item and then selects all the others systematically after that. For example, the auditor might pick the fifth receivable on the list of trade receivables and then every fifth or tenth after that. (This can be described as interval sampling.)

(c) By **haphazard selection**. This is the approach most likely to allow audit bias to creep in. This is a method by which an auditor picks a sample with no structured technique (that is, what we would call 'at random' although human bias may reduce the mathematical randomness of the choice). It is crucial that you understand the difference between this type of sampling and 'random' sampling, outlined above.

(d) By **monetary unit sampling (MUS)**. This is a **value-weighted selection**, so (for example, in trade receivables) every nth £ is selected, rather than every nth receivable (also known as interval sampling). The benefit of MUS is that it tests all material items, meaning larger value items are more likely to be selected and therefore samples can be smaller.

(e) By **block selection**. This involves selecting a block of continuous items (for example, April's invoices out of a population of the year's invoices). This is rarely an appropriate sample technique, as April's invoices may have different characteristics from the rest of the year and are not therefore representative of the whole population (for example, if they were posted by a different staff member due to holiday).

Activity 9: Sampling (1)

The objective of a substantive test will determine the population from which the sample is selected.

Required

For each of the objectives set out below, select the population from which the sample should be selected.

Objective	Population
Obtain evidence that sales have not been understated	▼
Obtain evidence that sales have not been overstated	▼

Picklist

- Sales ledger
- Sales order

4.4 Confidence level

KEY TERM

> **Tolerable misstatement:** For **tests of control**, the tolerable misstatement is the maximum rate of deviation from a control that auditors are willing to accept in the population and still conclude that the preliminary assessment of control risk is valid. For **tests of detail** (or **substantive testing**), the tolerable misstatement is the maximum monetary error in an account balance or class of transactions that the auditor is willing to accept and still conclude that the financial statements are true and fair.

When using a sample, the auditor has to be sufficiently **confident** that the results given by a sample reflect the results that would be given by testing the whole population. Sampling, in many areas of the financial statements, is necessary because it is the only cost-effective way an audit can be performed (testing everything would take too long and be too expensive). The size of samples selected will be affected by the auditor's assessment of the **tolerable misstatement**.

If overall **risk of misstatement is high**, the auditor needs to be very confident that the results from a sample reflect the results that would come from the whole population. Consequently, **detection risk** needs to be reduced to an acceptably **low** level. This would **increase the size of the sample** that the auditor tests. All this is a matter of auditor judgement based on the risks of misstatements arising and materiality levels. This sort of judgement is taken at the planning stage and amended, if necessary, as the audit progresses and more facts come to light. It is taken by a senior member of the audit team and approved by the audit partner.

The auditing standards outline factors that impact on sample sizes, and these are summarised below.

Illustration 2: The effect of various factors on sample sizes for tests of control.

Factor	Effect on sample size for tests of controls
Increase in extent to which auditor intends to rely on controls	Increase – because the more reliance the auditor intends to place on controls, the greater the assurance that they are operating effectively needs to be
Increase in the tolerable rate of deviation	Decrease
Increase in the expected rate of deviation	Increase – because if auditors expect errors to exist, they need to test more as they need to be satisfied that actual misstatement is lower than tolerable misstatement
Increase in the auditor's desired level of assurance that actual rate of deviation ≤ tolerable rate of deviation	Increase – because the more assurance the auditor needs, the more items they need to test
Increase of number of sampling units	Negligible effect

(FRC, 2025e)

Illustration 3: The effect of various factors on sample sizes for substantive testing (tests of detail).

Factor	Effect on sample size for tests of details
Increase in auditor's assessment of the risk of material misstatement	Increase – because the higher inherent and control risk is, the lower detection risk needs to be (hence, more tests)
Increase in the use of other procedures at the same assertion	Decrease – because the auditor is obtaining assurance from the other procedures (for example, analytical procedures)
Increase in the auditor's desired level of assurance that actual misstatement ≤ tolerable misstatement	Increase – because the more assurance the auditor needs, the more items they need to test
Increase in tolerable misstatement	Decrease – because there is more chance of it being found in the sample
Increase in expected misstatement	Increase – because if auditors expect more errors to exist, they need to test more as they need to be satisfied that actual misstatement is lower than tolerable misstatement
Stratification of the population	Decrease
Number of sampling units in population	Negligible effect

(FRC, 2025e)

Activity 10: Sampling (2)

Determination of sample sizes on an audit is a matter of judgement.

Required

Select the impact the following matters have on the sample sizes for tests of control.

Matters	Impact
Auditors intend to increase reliance on the company's system of internal control for the purposes of the audit.	▼
Auditors believe that there is likely to be a higher deviation rate in controls due to a new member of staff.	▼
Increased activity in the factory and new customers, resulting in 25% more sales invoices being issued during the year.	▼

Picklist

- Decrease
- Increase
- No effect

4.5 Advantages and disadvantages of different sampling methods

Sampling method	Advantages	Disadvantages
Block	Useful if interrogating a defined group of data ...	... but ignores the characteristics of data from outside that block (such as seasonal variations)
Haphazard	This non-statistical technique is good for targeting your sample ...	... but can still generate a biased and non-representative sample
Judgemental	Also good for targeting specific areas of the population ...	... but again, can lead to the selection of a non-representative sample through some form of bias
Random	Eliminates bias by relying on a mathematically selected sample	Requires IT expertise or the use of specialist maths tables to generate the sample
Stratified	Allows a broad range of items to be tested within the sample	Can lead to larger or more complex samples being selected which in turn may take longer to complete
Systematic	Ignores patterns and treats every item of the population the same way, eliminating bias	Still requires some judgement to determine the starting position and sampling interval so still may not be fully representative

(FRC, 2025e)

Chapter summary

- Auditors require evidence in order to be able to form an opinion on the financial statements. This is collected using a series of different activities (AEEIOUR):
  - Analytical procedures
  - Enquiry
  - External confirmation
  - Inspection
  - Observation
  - Recalculation
  - Reperformance
- Tests of control are used to verify the operating effectiveness of accounting systems and use all the techniques listed above (AEEIOUR) apart from analytical procedures and external confirmation. They should only be used when there are suitably robust controls in place to be tested – otherwise, substantive procedures should be used instead.
- Substantive testing includes substantive analytical procedures and should always be used on an audit – however, in the absence of testing controls, an audit should be conducted on a substantive basis alone. These are also known as tests of detail.
- Auditors require sufficient (enough) appropriate (both relevant and reliable) audit evidence to form their opinion. Relevance is determined by using assertions (occurrence, completeness, accuracy, cut-off, classification/understandability, existence, rights and obligations, valuation and allocation, and presentation) and specific audit procedures must be used to test each of these.
- Digital techniques in auditing are used to streamline the audit and allow for greater amounts of data to be tested with improved accuracy. They can include audit software run by the auditor and test data provided by the client. Recent advances in technology have allowed auditors to deploy data analytic tools, in order to analyse whole sets of data and use their findings to draw more accurate conclusions from their work.
- Sampling allows the auditor to gain assurance over large populations of data by selecting suitable samples for analysis. There are statistical and non-statistical techniques used and, in each case, care must be taken to ensure the right population is selected and the correct conclusions drawn. Each of these techniques has advantages and disadvantages that the auditor needs to be aware of when selecting the most appropriate sample for their testing.

Activity answers

Activity 1: Controls and tests – purchases

Any five from the following:

Controls	Tests of control
Necessity for orders is evidenced prior to ordering and a requisition is raised.	Review a sample of requisitions. Enquire about reorder levels with stores manager.
The company has a policy for choosing suppliers.	Review a sample of orders to ensure that the suppliers appear on the approved supplier list.
Goods received are examined for quantity and quality.	Observe the stores manager receiving some goods.
Goods received are checked against the order.	Observe the stores manager receiving some goods. For those goods, scrutinise a sample of orders for evidence of the check.
Supplier invoices are checked to the order.	Observe the accounts assistant checking supplier invoices to the relevant order.
Supplier invoices are checked for prices; quantities and calculations are given a reference number.	Scrutinise a sample of supplier invoices for evidence of these checks.
Cheque requests are presented for approval with supporting documentation.	Scrutinise paid invoices for any evidence of approval. Observe the cheque payments routine.
Supplier statements are reconciled to the purchase ledger.	Scrutinise a sample of reconciliations. How are differences dealt with?
The purchase ledger control account is regularly reconciled with the purchase ledger list of balances.	Scrutinise a sample of reconciliations. Establish how differences are dealt with.

Activity 2: Controls and tests – payroll

Any four of the following:

Controls	Tests of control
Pieces worked are recorded.	Review records of pieces worked and test for accuracy.
Pieces worked are reviewed.	Scrutinise the exception report and look for evidence of authorisation of extra production.
Payroll is prepared using an automated system.	Access payroll systems and confirm controls in existence (eg for new starters, attempt to add a fictitious member of staff to the payroll).
Identity of staff is verified prior to cash payments being made.	Attend a wages payout and observe the controls in operation.

Controls	Tests of control
The exception report should identify uplifts for a member of staff of more than 20% based on their weekly average wages (over a year).	Review wages paid over a sample period for staff with a 20% increase and confirm this was recorded by the exception report.
Bank transfers, in respect of payroll, are made to the correct employee.	Compare a sample of automatic bank transfers made with bank account details provided by employees.
Monthly salaries are paid to employee's own bank account.	For a sample of monthly salaries paid, confirm the bank account where salary is transferred matches the details held on file for that employee.

Activity 3: Controls or substantive?

Audit test	Test of control or substantive test?
Selection of ten invoices to test for correct authorisation in line with official signatory list	Test of control
Tracing ten non-current assets back to initial purchases invoices to verify their value	Substantive test
Tracing ten non-current assets back to initial purchases invoices to verify they have been allocated to the correct cost centre by the accounts clerk	Test of control

As you can see from the last two examples, the same audit test can have both controls and substantive purposes behind them – this comes out of effective and efficient audit planning.

Activity 4: Ginger Ltd

(a) Number of nights open during the year

Working

Substantive analytical procedures are used to verify an amount in total, so for Ginger 10 × 55% × £75 × 100 × 365 nights = £15,056,250 which proves the £15 million revenue figure reported is materially correct.

The other pieces of information may be useful but will not help (we are told that £75 includes all charges, so bar and restaurant spend are not required). Plus, you cannot just assume 365 nights a year as there may have been closures in some of them during the year (hence, the 'no further information required' option is inappropriate).

(b)

Findings	Implications
The room rate of £50 now means that the revenue for Ginger should only be around £10 million – the financial statements are still recording £15 million.	The reported amount for revenue may be misstated. There may be elements of revenue that we are unaware of – we will need to perform further testing on revenue to ensure there are no flaws in any other assumptions (eg occupancy rate). We may have to consider the danger that management are attempting to manipulate the financial statements and should consider their integrity. We should inspect management accounts to verify the amounts recorded for revenue on a monthly basis. We may need to enquire whether there are any hotel premises or income streams that we were unaware of and establish if this changes any of our risk assessments or materiality calculations.

Activity 5: Mixed audit approach or substantive procedures only?

Scenario	Approach
Scoot Ltd is a new company that has not been audited before and is dominated by its managing director and his informal operating style. Sales are of greatest importance to him as the company attempts to break into a competitive retail sector.	Substantive procedures only, with no tests of control
Whitney plc is an established listed company that operates in a stable market with strong governance procedures, including an audit committee.	Tests of control and substantive procedures
The board of Marine Ltd has just informed its external auditor that it wishes to replace its ledger systems due to a number of errors identified in its management accounts.	Substantive procedures only, with no tests of control

Tutorial note. This is not straightforward, but if the client is going to replace their systems, it is likely that they cannot currently be relied upon and therefore a purely substantive approach would be appropriate.

Activity 6: Assertions (1)

Audit test	
Select a sample of vehicles from the list of non-current assets and obtain their certificates of ownership.	Rights and obligations
Select a sample of receivables from the statement of financial position and agree to original invoices.	Existence
Select a sample of receivables from the sales ledger and agree to the final amount on the statement of financial position.	Completeness
Trace a selection of payments included in cost of sales to original invoices.	Occurrence

For the first audit test, seeking evidence of **ownership** proves that the entity has the right to include such assets within the financial statements (as well as any obligations that ownership would impose, such as maintenance).

The direction of testing is important in the next audit test – you are testing **from the receivables in the financial statements to their source** (the original sales invoices), which is a test that the figures exist (hence, testing for any overstatement of assets).

The direction of testing is important again for the third audit test – you are now testing **from the source to the financial statements,** which is a test that sales ledger balances selected have been included within the receivables figure in the financial statements. This helps to give comfort that receivables are complete (hence testing for any understatement of assets).

Note. In a real set of financial statements, you would not be able to see an individual receivables balance named on the statement of financial position as that level of detail is not required. In practice, you would test from the invoices to the receivables control account and then reconcile the control account total to the amount in the statement of financial position.

The final test is for overstatement but this time it is for a **transaction.** We want to make sure the transaction **occurred**. It is worth remembering that statement of profit or loss items are tested for occurrence while assets and liabilities are tested for existence (both can be reviewed for completeness when testing understatement).

Tutorial note. There are **exceptions** to the logic of specifying the direction of testing which relate to testing **negative** items such as credit notes.

For example, when **testing revenue**, the auditor would test from the source (invoice) to the financial records (revenue) for completeness or understatement because if an invoice was not present in the total, revenue would be understated or incomplete.

However, if **tracing a sample of credit notes to the revenue balance in the financial records,** this would actually be a test of existence or overstatement because if the credit note was not part of the total when it should be, the revenue balance would be overstated.

Activity 7: Assertions (2)

Situation	Procedure
Testing cut-off for staff bonuses paid at the end of the financial year	Verifying bonus payments to payroll records to determine their timing
Confirming the accuracy of staff bonuses paid at the end of the financial year	Reconciling payroll records to a schedule of staff bonus payments authorised by the finance director
Confirming the value of cash investments held in a savings account by a client	Obtaining a letter from the bank stating the amount of savings held by the client

Activity 8: Digital techniques in auditing

Procedure	Technique
Extraction of all receivables balances older than 120 days to perform irrecoverable receivable work	Audit software
Input of purchases invoices with false customer numbers to ensure that the system rejects the invoices	Test data
Comparison of suppliers on ledger with previous years to discover any new or missing suppliers	Audit software
Interrogation of a year's transactions to analyse profitability by product and store for a retailer	Data analytic tools

Activity 9: Sampling (1)

Objective	Population
Obtain evidence that sales have not been understated	Sales order
Obtain evidence that sales have not been overstated	Sales ledger

Activity 10: Sampling (2)

Matters	Impact
Auditors intend to increase reliance on the company's system of internal control for the purposes of the audit.	Increase
Auditors believe that there is likely to be a higher deviation rate in controls due to a new member of staff.	Increase
Increased activity in the factory and new customers, resulting in 25% more sales invoices being issued during the year.	No effect

Test your learning

1 When designing further audit procedures as a result of risk assessment, auditors design tests which give evidence about financial statement assertions.

Required

Select which category each assertion is relevant to.

Assertion	Category
Existence	▼
Accuracy, valuation and allocation	▼
Cut-off	▼

Picklist

- Account balances
- Classes of transaction

2 **Select which ONE of the following statements is the important general rule concerning audit sampling by ticking the appropriate box.**

	✓
All sampling units should have an equal chance of being selected for testing.	
All audit areas must be subject to sampling.	
Auditors must always stratify a population to focus attention on high value items.	
The more items there are in a population, the higher the sample sizes must be.	

3 When using sampling techniques, auditors must select a sample such that each individual sampling unit is capable of being selected.

Required

Select which method of sampling will be most suitable in each instance described.

Instance	Method
Simran has been asked to select a sample of 12 sales invoices to trace from sales order to general ledger. There are 16 folders of sales orders for the year, stored in the sales office.	▼
Julie has been asked to select a sample of 5 purchase ledger accounts to carry out a supplier statement reconciliation. There are 16 purchase ledger accounts.	▼
Ben is selecting a sample of inventory lines to perform a valuation test. The audit team have been instructed to use the computerised techniques available to them, one of which is a sample selection program.	▼

Picklist

- Haphazard
- Random
- Systematic

4 Determination of sample sizes on an audit is a matter of judgement.

Required

Select the impact the following matters have on the sample sizes for audit tests.

Matters	Impact
Increase in the auditor's assessment of the risk of material misstatement	▼
Increase in tolerable misstatement	▼
Decision to stratify a large population	▼

Picklist

- Decrease
- Increase
- No effect

5 **Complete the following statement on digital techniques in auditing.**

Automated tools and techniques are methods of obtaining [▼] by using [▼]. [▼] is [▼] that can check [▼] on computer systems by [▼] or by comparing versions of [▼].

[▼] is a way of checking computer [▼] by inputting real or false information and observing how the program deals with it.

Picklist

- Audit software
- Computers
- Data
- Evidence
- Interrogating
- Programming
- Programs
- Software
- Test data

5 Substantive testing

Learning outcomes

Having studied this chapter, you will be able to:

5	**Understand procedures for obtaining sufficient and appropriate evidence**
5.1	**Audit assertions and audit procedures** Learners need to be able to: 5.1.3 identify suitable audit procedures to test financial statement transactions and balances: • non-current assets • inventory • receivables • cash and bank • borrowings • payables • provisions • revenue • purchases • payroll and other expenses

Assessment context

Although there is only one learning outcome listed here, it covers a lot of content and is likely to be assessed within Task 7 which could be worth up to 15 marks, so this topic is essential for you to engage with.

Qualification context

Most of this chapter will be application of terms previously seen in your AAT studies, although the use of some terms may not initially be clear. Try to refer to previous units if there are elements of terminology that you are unfamiliar with.

Business context

Inventory and work in progress (WIP) often represent a significant asset on the statement of financial position, with the value of inventory also having a direct impact on profit. A considerable amount of audit effort is usually devoted to this area because of these factors – talk to any seasoned audit professional and they will usually have the most engaging stories to tell about either the nature of an inventory count (eg smoked haddock stored in a cold, draughty shed) or the timing (eg 6am on New Year's Day!).

The audit of other assets is often a major part of the audit for an auditor, as it usually requires significant work on valuation and existence to counter the risk of overstated amounts. Given the nature of the agency problem that we covered earlier, it is entirely possible that the directors of an entity may try to make their company seem as big as possible, meaning that auditors will usually have their work cut out for them.

The audit of liabilities is quite a change for the auditor – instead of being on the lookout for overstated assets used to bolster a potentially fragile statement of financial position, you are now faced with the possibility of items being either understated or even ignored. Remember that visibility (or rather lack of it) is the biggest audit risk here – the collapses of large companies such as Carillion in 2018 and even Enron back in 2001 were partly due to the impact of liabilities that were not appropriately recognised.

Chapter overview

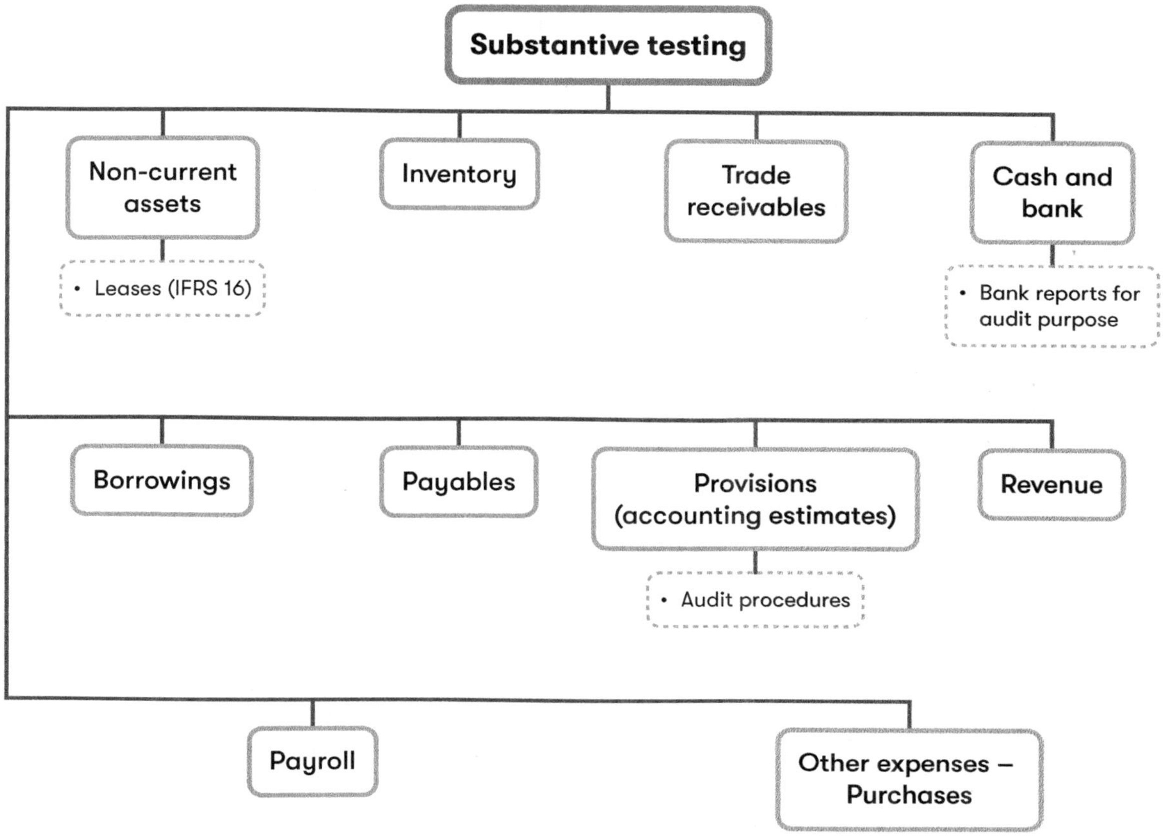

Introduction

The primary focus of this chapter is to prepare you for tasks which test your ability to state what you are doing and why you are doing it. This could include risk assessments and specific audit procedures that could require knowledge of various parts of the financial statements.

The accounting knowledge required for such written tasks will not be overly specific, allowing you to demonstrate your skills in describing what the auditor would actually do. There are many activities here you can use as valuable practice.

To assist you in producing answers to these activities, here is some guidance on how to write audit procedures.

Writing an audit procedure

Each audit procedure should state the following:

- What you are doing
- Why you are doing it
- How you are doing it
- Where you have to go to do it
- Who you need to see to do it
- What documentation you will need

Here is an example, showing each of these at work:

> Obtain a sample of sales invoices (What) from the sales ledger clerk (Who) in the finance department (Where) to confirm the correct price in each case (How) using current price lists (Documentation) to ensure the accuracy (Why) of the sales figures.

Procedures should always be specific and link to the purpose of the audit work being undertaken. Although you will not have to produce these in your assessment, knowing how they should be constructed is essential for you to understand how to audit the financial statements.

1 Non-current assets

KEY TERM

> **Non-current assets:** These are assets held for continuing use in the business.

We saw from earlier chapters that, for **assets** and **liabilities**, the relevant assertions are:

- Existence (overstatement)
- Completeness (understatement)
- Rights and obligations (or ownership)
- Accuracy, valuation and allocation (amount)
- Classification (which account)
- Presentation (disclosure)

We will now look at other items that are classified as either **assets** or **debit balances** (usually both, but not always). First is the asset balance that is usually the largest for an entity: **non-current assets**.

An important test when reviewing non-current assets is to ensure that only **capital expenditure** is included on the statement of financial position.

Activity 1: JICS driving school

You are the audit senior working on the audit of JICS driving school. You are testing non-current assets for overstatement (existence). Based on your review of the non-current assets register, you have noted that it includes the items listed below.

Required

Identify four items from the following list that you do not believe to be capital in nature.

	✓
10 × Ford Fiestas	
2 × PCs and monitors for the office	
2 × desk telephones	
10 × mobile telephones	
Car insurance	
Car servicing	
Installation of dual controls in cars	
Replacement tyre for car no. 6	
Repairs to bumper of car no. 4	
Office fixtures and fittings	
'JICS' signs to go on top of cars	

Activity 2: Campey Ltd non-current assets

Below is a schedule of non-current assets at Campey Ltd.

	Land £	Buildings £	Vehicles £	Fittings £	Total £
Cost at 1 October 20X8	1,000,000	3,500,000	60,000	125,150	4,685,150
Additions	–	–	15,000	800	15,800
Disposals	–	–	–	–	–
Cost at 30 November 20X9	1,000,000	3,500,000	75,000	125,950	4,700,950
Accumulated depreciation at 1 October 20X8	–	140,000	26,250	37,545	203,795
Depreciation charge	–	70,000	12,188	18,893	101,081
Accumulated depreciation at 30 November 20X9	–	210,000	38,438	56,438	304,876
Carrying amount at 30 November 20X9	1,000,000	3,290,000	36,562	69,512	4,396,074
Carrying amount at 1 October 20X8	1,000,000	3,360,000	33,750	87,605	4,481,355

Required

Set out, in a manner suitable for inclusion in the audit plan, the audit procedures to be undertaken for each of the assertions below in order to ensure that non-current assets are fairly stated in the financial statements. You have already verified the opening balances to the prior year audit file.

- Completeness
- Rights and obligations
- Existence
- Accuracy, valuation and allocation

Note. Depreciation rates are 2% straight line for buildings, 25% diminishing balance for vehicles and 15% straight line for fittings.

1.1 Leases (IFRS 16)

Leases are studied in the Level 4 *Financial Accounting* unit. You do not need detailed knowledge of the financial reporting standard (IFRS 16, *Leases*) for this unit. However, you do need to understand the key risk associated with this item, which is that it may be materially misstated in the financial statements.

KEY TERM

Lease: A lease is a contract that allows an entity the right to use an asset for a period of time, in exchange for some kind of consideration.

The leased asset is referred to as a right-of-use asset. The entity that has the right to use this leased asset is known as the **lessee**. IFRS 16 requires **recognition of all leases** in the **lessee's statement of financial position except short-term leases** (those with a lease term of 12 months or less) and leases where the asset is of low value (taken on a case-by-case basis).

Illustration 1: Lease disclosure in the financial statements of lessees

The financial statements of a lessee will have the following headings in relation to a leased asset:

Statement of financial position (extract)

	£
Non-current assets	
Right-of-use asset	X
Non-current liabilities	
Lease liability	X
Current liabilities	
Lease liability	X
	X

Statement of profit or loss and other comprehensive income (extract)

	£
Depreciation charge (in relevant expense category)	X
Finance charges	X

Audit risk for leases

Auditors must test leased items to verify that they are correctly accounted for in line with IFRS 16. This might include the following issues:

- **Recognition** of an asset as a right-of-use asset when it **does not qualify** (such as short term or low value leases, or any that do not satisfy the criteria from IFRS 16, such as control or identification)
- **Non-recognition** of a leased asset which **should be classified as a right-of-use asset**
- **Material misstatement** in the accounting treatment of a right-of-use asset (such as incorrect calculation of any lease assets or liabilities, or the amount to be charged in depreciation)
- **Incorrect classification** between current and non-current lease liabilities

2 Inventory

KEY TERM

Inventory: Sub-classified as raw materials, work in progress (WIP) and finished goods.

The audit approach for **inventory** must include the three main elements of inventory balances seen in the statement of financial position: **quantity**, **valuation** and **disclosure**.

One audit test in particular gives evidence in relation to **completeness, rights and obligations** (ie ownership) and **existence**. This test is **attending the physical inventory count** carried out by the entity being audited and it provides evidence of inventory **quantity**. It can also provide **corroborative evidence** of the likely **valuation** of such an asset due to recording information about the **condition** of inventory as well.

There are **three methods** for an entity to physically count its inventory:

- **Year-end count**, where the entire inventory of the entity is counted as close to the reporting period end as possible to provide a figure for the closing inventory balance
- **Interim count** with follow through to year end – as above, but the count occurs during the year and all items both inwards and outwards are reconciled to arrive at a calculated amount
- **Continuous inventory records and perpetual inventory** – an automated system records all items inwards and outwards, and maintains an ongoing balance of inventory at any one time – this is tested periodically as part of the entity's normal controls assessment

The auditor will attend the entity's physical inventory count to verify inventory quantities but **it is not the auditor's responsibility to count the inventory**. This is carried out as part of the legal responsibilities of the management of the entity to keep accounting records in line with the **Companies Act 2006**.

Quantity

The most common method for the auditor to gain evidence as to the **amount** of inventory held at the end of the reporting period is to attend the year-end inventory count.

Activity 3: Paper Products Ltd

You are the senior on the audit of Paper Products Ltd. Your client imports paper from Scandinavia and supplies it to major publishers and stationery suppliers in the UK. A new team member will be attending the annual inventory count this Saturday. It is your responsibility to brief her on how she should prepare for the count and what she should do when she is there.

Required

List the points you will cover during your briefing with the new team member. You may wish to think about what you would need to consider before the count, during the count and after the count has taken place.

Activity 4: Inventory assertions

Consider each of the following tests plus results from the audit file recording attendance at the annual inventory count of Glad Rags. From the picklist below, select the most appropriate assertion for that test.

Test	Assertion
Test Form an opinion of the condition of inventory and record any instances of damage or obsolescence. **Result** There were 15 × 10m rolls of fabric stored near the roof of the warehouse where birds had nested, making the fabric unusable.	▼
Test Trace 10 × 10m rolls of fabric from the inventory sheets to the relevant shelves of the warehouse. **Result** All 10 rolls were found on the shelves in the locations specified by the main accounting system.	▼
Test Trace 10 × 10m rolls of fabric from the relevant shelves of the warehouse to the inventory sheets. **Result** All 10 rolls were traced back to the list generated by the main accounting system.	▼
Test Confirm that the fabric and garments held in the secure off-site storage facility are to be included in Glad Rags' inventory balance by verifying them to supporting documentation and invoices. **Result** All rolls of fabric and garments were traced back to storage invoices and haulage records, confirming that they belong to Glad Rags.	▼

Picklist

- Accuracy, valuation and allocation
- Completeness
- Existence
- Rights and obligations

Valuation

Once quantity is established by attending the entity's count, the next characteristic of inventory must be assessed – **valuation**. Inventory must be valued at the **lower** of **cost** and **net realisable value (NRV)** in order to comply with IAS 2 *Inventories*. The auditor will therefore need to design procedures that establish amounts for each for this comparison to occur.

Activity 5: Valuing inventory

Your firm is the external auditor of William Ltd. William Ltd owns a grocery store in a small town. You are responsible for planning the procedures to be undertaken to test the valuation of inventories in the financial statements for the year ended 31 March 20X4. An inventory listing will be prepared as at 31 March 20X4, listing the products held at the year end, the number of each type of product and their cost.

Required

Set out, in a manner suitable for inclusion in the audit plan, the audit procedures to be undertaken to test the valuation of the inventory figure in the financial statements for the year ended 31 March 20X4.

Note. **You do not need to discuss audit procedures undertaken at the year-end in relation to the inventory count.**

Other audit tests for inventory

We saw the use of **accounting estimates** mentioned in the solution to the previous activity when discussing the possible impact on the NRV of supermarket inventory of items going literally '**past their shelf life**'. Such a loss requires a degree of **judgement** by the entity's management and the auditor needs to establish whether their conclusion is **reasonable** or not. Similar estimates are also required for valuing items of **raw materials, work in progress** (WIP) and **finished goods**.

We must not forget that the auditor reviews not only the **amounts** included in the financial statements but also the way they are **presented** and **disclosed** – **classification** is the appropriate assertion here and the auditor will make sure that the relevant disclosure requirements are followed. Typically, disclosure includes:

- **Accounting policies** used in calculating things such as cost and NRV are fully disclosed
- Ensuring that inventory is **sub-classified as raw materials, WIP, and finished goods**

Raw materials

Raw materials are tested to ensure that they are **held at cost**. This is because it is extremely unlikely that NRV would differ from cost for raw materials, unless they had been damaged or the value was affected by age.

First, auditors must understand how the company determines the cost of raw materials.

The company might be able to identify each item separately, in which case they can be valued at their own original cost.

However, it will not be possible to value some inventory in this way because of the nature of it, and the company will have to use a technique, such as first in first out (FIFO) which you should be aware of.

Work in progress (WIP)

You should know that accounting standards define cost as **cost of purchase plus the cost of conversion.**

The cost of conversion becomes relevant when considering WIP and finished goods. It will include:

- **Directly attributable costs** (for example, labour, machine costs)
- Other **production costs** (for example, lighting in the factory)

The auditors will need to test the company's calculation of cost of conversion. In general terms, the auditors may apply analytical procedures (for example, comparing similar inventory lines from this year to last year to see if any changes in price appear reasonable).

The allocation of **production overheads** must be done on the basis of normal activity, and the auditors must ensure that the overall calculations are reasonable.

Finished goods

Finished goods are most likely to be affected by **NRV**, as there is a market for them. WIP might also be affected by NRV, but this would be more difficult to judge.

NRV is the estimated or actual selling price of the goods.

The auditors should ensure any goods they noted as being obsolete or damaged at the inventory count have been reduced in value.

Activity 6: Hodgson Ltd

The following are extracts from the books and records of Hodgson Ltd, a manufacturer of garden equipment.

Required

Identify the audit work to be performed on these inventory balances, both individually and in aggregate.

	£
Raw materials	164,810
Work in progress	55,000
Finished goods	117,000
	336,810

Cut-off

Given the **sensitivity** of **statement of profit or loss items** like profit and cost of sales to recorded amounts of inventory, the main aim of the auditor is to ensure that there is **consistency** over **when** an amount of inventory is either purchased or sold. The aim is to apply the **matching concept**, especially at the very start and end of the reporting period to ensure inclusion in the correct year.

The rule is that income and expense is recorded at the point where the **risks** and **rewards** of ownership of that item are **transferred** (ie based on movement of inventory). The diagram below shows the treatment of items **in the financial statements for the year end** for items **sold** and **purchased** both **before** the year end and afterwards.

Illustration 2: Inventory cut-off

	Before ← **Year end**	→ After
Revenues	**Goods Despatched Note (GDN)** Included in: • Revenue ✓ • Receivables ✓ • Inventory ×	**Goods Despatched Note (GDN)** Included in: • Revenue × • Receivables × • Inventory ✓
Purchases	**Goods Received Note (GRN)** Included in: • Purchases ✓ • Payables ✓ • Inventory ✓	**Goods Received Note (GRN)** Included in: • Purchases × • Payables × • Inventory ×

Cut-off tests for revenue

(a) Obtain last GDN number at year end

(b) Select a sample of GDNs raised before and after the year end, and ensure the revenue is accounted for in the correct period. Select a sample of sales invoices posted before and after the year end and ensure that GDNs are raised in the same period

Cut-off tests for purchases

As for revenues, but replace GDN with GRN and sales invoice with purchase invoice.

Activity 7: Cut-off testing

It is now the final audit of Glad Rags. The inventory cut-off information obtained by your audit firm at the inventory count is given below. The audit junior has obtained follow-up information to establish whether cut-off is correct but is unsure what conclusion they should draw.

Client:	Glad Rags Ltd		**Prepared by/Date:**	A Junior 2/1/X5
Reporting date:	30 November 20X4		**Reviewed by/Date:**	

Inventory cut-off

Last deliveries out of the warehouse on 30/11/X4:

Sales order/GDN	Customer	Agreed to November Sales Day Book
200894/GDN 12403	J Club Ltd	✔
200895/GDN 12404	IZK Ltd	✔
200896/GDN 12405	Ginger Ltd	✔

The above revenue items have all been excluded from the inventory count and a receivable exists. I reviewed GDN 12406 to 12415 inclusive and all were included in the December Sales Day Book.

Last deliveries into the warehouse on 30/11/X4:

Purchase order/GRN	Supplier	Agreed to November Purchases Day Book
100552/GRN 1013	Fine Fabrics Ltd	✔
100553/GRN 1014	Fine Fabrics Ltd	✔
100554/GRN 1015	Terry's Threads	×

All the above purchase items were included in the inventory count but payables for Fine Fabrics only have been created at the year end. GRNs 1016 to 1025 inclusive were all included in the December Purchases Day Book.

The invoice for order 100554 was not received until 15 December and was included in December's Purchases Day Book. The value was £52,476. Terry's Threads has been included in the new year payables balance – the senior accountant explained that this was a regular order that arrived early.

Required

Advise the junior whether they should refer the results of their revenue and purchases cut-off tests to their supervisor or not by highlighting the appropriate action. Materiality has been set at £50,000.

	No further action ✓	Refer to supervisor ✓
Revenues cut-off testing:		
Purchases cut-off testing:		

3 Trade receivables

KEY TERM

Trade receivables: The amount owed by customers in respect of credit sales.

Circularisation: A specific technique used to test the receivables balance by writing directly to customers owing money to the audited entity and asking them to confirm what they believe they owe.

Circularisation results can be used to compare against the records held by the entity of sums owed by that customer and any discrepancies reconciled.

Illustration 3: Circularisation is conducted as follows:

(a) Obtain a **listing** of trade receivables, as at the year end.

(b) **Agree the total** to sales ledger control account in the nominal ledger.

(c) **Review** the listing for any obvious **omissions** or **misstatements**.

(d) Select a **sample** of receivables accounts for **positive confirmation**. The letter should be on the **client's headed notepaper**, signed by the client with a copy of the current statement attached. It should request that the **reply** is **sent directly to the auditor** and reply-paid envelopes should be included.

(e) After a **reasonable period**, the auditor should send **follow-up** requests by post.

(f) If responses are still not forthcoming, then these should be followed up by **emails** and **phone calls**.

(g) The auditor should **investigate** any **disputed balances**.

(h) Often a **50% response rate** is the best that the auditor can ever hope for, but all **reasonable efforts** should be made to agree those receivables sampled where no reply is forthcoming. This is achieved by confirmation of individual outstanding invoices or alternative procedures such as verifying outstanding items to back up documentation, reviewing any cash received from that customer after the year end and discussions with the entity's credit controller.

It is worth noting that circularisation is usually only a good test of **existence** and **rights and obligations**. It **does not test accuracy, valuation and allocation**, as most customers will not confirm if the balance is understated, and agreeing that a debt is owed does not provide evidence that the debt will be settled.

A specimen receivables circularisation letter is given below:

WOODRIGHT LTD
24/26 Arthur Road
Newcastle upon Tyne
NT1 4LJ

To: Rossney & Co.
327 Skelworth Road
Aberdeen
AB11 4PR

Account: 107507

5 January 20X8
Our ref: TCO/PJM/AUD

Dear Sir(s)

The balance on your account in our books at 31 December 20X7 is £74,329.28 due from you.

We would be grateful if, for audit purposes, you could confirm your agreement of this balance by completing, signing and returning this form in the enclosed pre-paid envelope direct to our auditors, Tish & Co., Arlott House, 1 Wicket Lane, London NW1 3RT.

Remittances in settlement of amounts due should not be sent to our auditors.

If you cannot agree the balance, will you please note on the form the amount outstanding according to your records, together with such details you can provide of the differences. We shall be grateful for your co-operation in this matter.

Yours faithfully

PJ Marsh

The balance at 31/12/X7 (date) stated above is (please tick one box):

Agreed ☐

Not agreed and the position according to our records is set out here ☑

Invoice not yet received for – £12,454.33
∴ Balance agreed = £61,874.95

Signed PE Carr Date 3/2/X8

On behalf of Rossney & Co.

Activity 8: Circularisation

You are continuing your work at Glad Rags Ltd. The receivables circularised at the year-end are listed below, along with information on the responses you have received and supporting information from Glad Rags. The reporting date is 30 November 20X4.

Sample selected from sales ledger

	Amount owed per sales ledger	Response from customer	Other information supplied by customer
British Clothes Stores plc	484,536	439,598	Cheque in post
IZK Ltd	74,973	74,973	n/a
Tisco Stores plc	78,805	71,663	Disputed invoice
J Club Ltd	323,024	323,024	n/a
Cavanaghs Ltd	14,388	nil	Goods not received yet
H and T Ltd	18,933	nil	Cheques in post
Nice Clothes Ltd	17,231	nil	Cheques in post
Ginger Ltd	22,315	22,315	n/a

Cash book extracts (receipts)

Date	Details	Amount £
1 December 20X4	BCS sales ledger	44,938
10 December 20X4	H and T sales ledger	8,934
14 December 20X4	Nice Clothes sales ledger	7,392
12 January 20X4	H and T sales ledger	9,999
18 January 20X4	Nice Clothes sales ledger	9,839

Glad Rags warehouse despatch information

GDN 12398	28/11/20X4	British Clothes Stores plc	£23,399
GDN 12399	28/11/20X4	Value Mart plc	£12,778
GDN 12400	29/11/20X4	Cavanaghs Ltd	£14,388
GDN 12401	29/11/20X4	Tisco Stores plc	£78,805

Required

Using all the information given above, decide which of these balances requires referral to your supervisor.

Illustration 4: Other standard audit tests for receivables

Audit objective		Example tests	
(a)	Completeness/existence	(i)	Obtain **listing** of trade receivables and **reconcile** to nominal ledger.
		(ii)	Check details of **despatches** of goods around the year end and ensure they are correctly treated (ie recorded in the correct period for cut-off).
		(iii)	Check that a **sales invoice** has been raised for all despatches during the year.
		(iv)	Review after date **credit notes** issued.
(b)	Rights and obligations	(i)	Trace a sample of trade receivables to **cash received post year end**.
		(ii)	**Discuss** with management and/or review **board minutes** to establish whether any trade receivables have been **factored**.
(c)	Accuracy, valuation and allocation	(i)	Review **consistency** of **policy** and its appropriateness.
		(ii)	Discuss significant **overdue debts** with a company official using a trade receivables **aged analysis**.
		(iii)	Review relevant **correspondence**.
		(iv)	Ensure all debts **written off** were properly authorised.
		(v)	Review allocation of after-date cash received.
(d)	Presentation	(i)	Ensure trade receivables are appropriately **categorised** within current assets.
		(ii)	Ensure **classification** is correct as per Companies Act 2006 (trade receivables, other receivables, prepayments).

Activity 9: Pond Ltd

You are the audit senior on the audit of Pond Ltd, a gemstone dealer.

Sales ledger listing

	£
Affectionado Ltd	76,002
Astra Stones Ltd	Nil
B. Trow Ltd	34,726
Bea Myan Ltd	7,013
Crystal Eyes plc	12,997
Engagement Centre Ltd	16,821
Gemba-Gems Ltd	22,032
Gemeyma Ltd	17,152
Jewels 'r' Us Ltd (> 90 days overdue)	3,294
Love Me Tender Ltd	6,111
Magnifique Ltd (> 60 days overdue)	987
Moonglow Ltd	1,342
Pearly Kween Ltd	812
Ruby-Dubie Ltd	467
Ring-ring Ltd	12,142
Wed-Me Ltd	(8,429)
	203,469

Required

Assuming that the largest balances will be selected, identify four other items from the sales ledger listing above that you would review, giving reasons for your selection.

4 Cash and bank

KEY TERM

Cash and bank: Includes all bank accounts held by the entity as well as any cash amounts held on site (such as petty cash and till floats).

The key audit test performed in the area of cash and bank is a review of the audited entity's **bank reconciliation**.

KEY TERM

Bank reconciliation: A process designed to understand the timing differences between the entity's cash book and the bank's understanding of the entity's bank balance.

Activity 10: Bank reconciliation

You are the audit junior and have been given the bank reconciliation for the year ended 31 December 20X6 for Glad Rags.

Bank reconciliation for Glad Rags as at 31 December 20X6

		£	£
Balance per cash book			52,296.62
Balance per statement			54,501.00
Less unpresented cheques			
	Cheque number:		
	010	7,834.53	
	695	19,721.87	
	696	17.98	
			(27,574.38)
Add outstanding lodgements			
	Lodgement number:		
	095	15,000.00	
	097	10,000.00	
			25,000.00
Add bank error			1,000.00
			52,926.62

Required

(a) Identify and describe the audit procedures that you should perform on the bank reconciliation.

(b) Select any item(s) that you would refer to the audit supervisor from your review.

	✓
Bank error	
Items to be written off	
Arithmetic	
Disclosure items	
Errors with source data	

Illustration 5: Tests for cash and bank

Other than reviewing the bank reconciliation, other tests for cash and bank include:

	Audit objective		Example tests
(a)	Completeness/existence	(i)	Obtain listing of bank and cash balances and reconcile to nominal ledger.
		(ii)	Review bank confirmation letter for details of all accounts held.
		(iii)	Count petty cash balance.
		(iv)	Review cashbook for unusual items.
(b)	Rights and obligations	(i)	Review bank letter to ensure valid title to accounts held.
(c)	Presentation	(i)	Review bank letter for any legal right to set off.
		(ii)	Investigate whether any accounts are secured over assets of the company.

4.1 Bank reports for audit purposes

The practice of obtaining **certificates** or **reports** from banks is an important feature in the proper discharge of the auditors' responsibilities. The **difficulty** for the auditor is getting hold of information regarding their client from a **third party** with whom they have **no direct contractual relationship**. The practice note sets out how both sides should act in this regard.

Procedures

- A standard letter should be sent in duplicate on each occasion by the auditor on their own note paper to each bank branch that the client holds an account at, or has had dealings with, since the end of the previous accounting period.
- Auditors should ensure that the bank receives their client's authority to permit disclosure of such information to a third party.

Contents of the letter

The **core information** requested in the standard letter is as follows:

(a) Bank accounts and balances:
  - Including details of any **restrictions** on accounts for balances
  - Including details of **accounts closed** during the period

(b) Details of **set-off arrangements**

(c) **Loans, overdrafts** and **associated covenants, guarantees** and **indemnities**, including term and repayment frequency

(d) **Securities** charged with reference to items listed above

(e) **Other banks** or **branches** where the customer has established a relationship during the period

The **supplementary information** requested in the **bank letter** is as follows:

(a) Trade finance:
  - **Bills** discounted with recourse
  - Any **guarantees, bonds** or **indemnities** given to the bank by the customer on behalf of **third parties**
  - Other **contingent liabilities.**

(b) Securities

5 Borrowings

KEY TERM

> **Non-current liabilities:** Loans repayable at a date more than one year after the year end. Examples include bank loans and debentures (generally known as borrowings).

Auditors are concerned with completeness, accuracy, valuation and allocation and presentation.

Completeness

- Obtain/prepare a schedule of loans outstanding at the end of the reporting period
- Compare opening balances to the previous year's working papers (closing balances at the end of last year)
- Test the clerical accuracy of the schedule
- Compare balances to the general ledger
- Check the names of lenders to relevant information (such as bank letter or register of debenture-holders)
- Review minutes and cash book to ensure that all loans have been recorded

Accuracy, valuation and allocation

- Trace additions and repayments to entries in the cash book
- Confirm repayments are in accordance with the loan agreement
- Examine receipts for loan repayments
- Obtain direct confirmation from lenders about amounts loaned and the terms thereof
- Verify interest charged for the period and the adequacy of accrued interest

Presentation

Review the disclosures made in the financial statements and ensure they meet legal requirements

Activity 11: HEC Ltd

You have noted on the bank letter that your client, HEC Ltd, has a mortgage which is repayable over 20 years.

Required

Set out, in a format suitable for inclusion in an audit plan, the audit procedures to be carried out on this loan.

6 Payables

KEY TERM

> **Payables:** These are amounts the company owes to its suppliers.

Trade and other payables might not individually be the largest credit balances on the statement of financial position (loans can sometimes be bigger) but there are still various tests that need to be performed on them as they may still be the largest credit balance on aggregate.

Activity 12: Gavilar Ltd

Gavilar Ltd as at 31 December 20X7 Statement of financial position (extract)	£
Trade payables	476,870
Other payables	123,600
	600,470

Required

Set out, in a manner suitable for inclusion in the audit plan, the audit procedures to be undertaken for each assertion in order to ensure that both trade and other payables are fairly stated in the financial statements of Gavilar Ltd.

7 Provisions (accounting estimates)

KEY TERM

> **Accounting estimate:** An approximation of the amount of an item in the absence of a precise means of measurement.

Examples include:

- Allowances to reduce inventories and receivables to their estimated realisable value
- Depreciation charges
- Accrued revenue
- Provision for a loss from a lawsuit
- Provision to meet warranty claims

A provision should be recognised when (i) a company has a **present obligation** (legal or constructive) where (ii) a **probable** outflow of resources embodying economic benefits will be necessary to settle it and (iii) that benefit can be **reliably estimated**.

Directors and management are responsible for making accounting estimates included in the financial statements. These estimates are often made in conditions of **uncertainty** regarding the outcome of events and involve the use of judgement. The risk of a material misstatement therefore increases when accounting estimates are involved (and thus inherent risk is higher). **Audit evidence** supporting accounting estimates is generally less than conclusive and so auditors need to exercise **significant judgement**.

Accounting estimates may be produced as part of the routine operations of the accounting system, or may be a non-routine procedure at the period end. Where, as is frequently the case, a **formula** based on past experience is used to calculate the estimate, it should be reviewed regularly by management (for example, actual vs estimate in prior periods).

7.1 Audit procedures

The auditors should gain an understanding of the procedures and methods used by management to make accounting estimates. This will aid the auditors' planning of their own procedures. Auditors must carry out at least one or more of the following procedures.

Step 1 Review and test the process

The auditors should:

- Evaluate the data and consider the assumptions on which the estimate is based
- Test the calculations involved in the estimate
- Compare estimates made for prior periods with actual results of those periods
- Consider management's/directors' review and approval procedures

Step 2 Use of an independent estimate

Such an estimate (made or obtained by the auditors) may be compared with the accounting estimate.

Step 3 Review of subsequent events

The auditors should review transactions or events after the period end which may reduce or even remove the need to test accounting estimates. For example, if directors have estimated an allowance for an irrecoverable debt, but all debt existing at the end of the reporting period has been paid by the date of the auditor's report, this provision will no longer be required.

8 Revenue

Revenue is often tested at the same time as **receivables**, due to it being the other side of the double entry. Revenue testing is usually done by **analytical procedures**: it should be possible to see **predictable relationships** arising.

Key assertions relating to revenue are completeness and accuracy. The auditor wants to confirm that all relevant revenue has been included and that revenue actually does relate to the correct year.

Completeness

Revenue is often tested by analytical procedures, as there is usually a great deal of information available in a company about its revenue and it should be possible to see predictable relationships arising.

Auditors should:

- Review the level of revenue over the year, comparing it on a month-by-month basis with previous years
- Consider the effect that any price rises have had on both the quantity of items sold and the amount of revenue received
- Consider the level of goods returned, sales allowances and discounts

In addition, the auditors may test the completeness of recording of revenue in the original records, for example, tracing from documents that first record revenue right through to the general ledger.

So, for example, the auditor may trace through from a sales order to a goods despatch note to a sales invoice to the sales day book to the sales ledger to the general ledger.

In a cash business, the auditor may trace from the till roll to the sales day book to the sales ledger to the general ledger.

Accuracy

The auditors should also check that revenue has been measured correctly by:

- Checking calculations and additions on sales invoices
- Ensuring VAT has been dealt with appropriately
- Checking discounts have been applied properly

- Checking the casting of the sales ledger accounts and control account

9 Payroll

When the auditors are scrutinising payroll-related payables, they may also carry out substantive procedures on payroll expense, which is highly likely to be **material** to the financial statements.

A great deal of testing may be done by **analytical procedures**, as there are a number of predictable relationships (number of staff, standard rates of pay, ratio of deductions to pay etc).

However, the auditor may also carry out **tests of detail** in relation to occurrence, measurement and completeness.

Occurrence

- Agree individual remuneration per payroll to personnel records
- Confirm existence of employees by visiting them
- Agree benefits paid to supporting documentation

Accuracy

- Recalculate benefits
- Recalculate deductions of tax and NI to confirm accuracy
- Confirm validity of other deductions, eg pension contributions to conditions of pension scheme

Completeness

- Agree a sample of employees from individual records to the payroll
- Confirm joiners have been paid in the correct month
- Confirm whether leavers have been correctly removed from payroll
- Recalculate amounts in the payroll
- Confirm payment of pay to bank transfer records
- Agree net pay per cash book to payroll
- Scrutinise payroll and investigate unusual items

10 Other expenses – Purchases

When testing purchases, auditors are concerned with whether they have occurred, whether they are measured correctly, and whether they have been made for valid business reasons.

We have already considered the issue of cut-off on purchases in relation to inventory.

Occurrence

The auditors often test purchases by using **analytical procedures**.

Auditors should:

- Consider the level of purchases on a month-by-month basis compared with previous years
- Consider the effect on value of purchases of price changes
- Consider the effect on value of purchases of changes in products purchased
- Compare the ratio of trade payables to purchases with previous years
- Compare the ratio of trade payables to inventory with previous years
- Consider the level of major expenses other than purchases in comparison with previous years

In addition, the auditors may test the completeness of recording of purchases in the original records – for example, tracing documents that first record purchases right through to the general ledger.

Also, to check the validity of purchases in the records, the auditors may test individual items in the nominal ledger back through the records to the original purchase order and requisition.

Activity 13: Adjustments

Indicate whether the following matters require to be adjusted or not.

Matter	Adjust?
The auditor has found an invoice for office supplies ordered and delivered on the last day of the financial year. The invoice amount has not been included in the total for purchases in the statement of profit or loss. The amount for these supplies is material.	▼
The auditor has completed analytical review of the cost of sales for a bakery. This analysis has indicated that ingredient costs per loaf have increased from 12.8 pence in the previous year to a figure closer to £3.56 per loaf. The non-financial information on the numbers of loaves has been corroborated during the audit.	▼
The auditor has selected 20 payments from the purchase ledger total and has been tracing them back to invoices for evidence of both existence and valuation. Of these 20 payments, 19 have been traced successfully back for both assertions. The 20th item has no invoice and relates to health and safety assessments carried out at the entity's head office. A similar amount was included in last year's statement of profit or loss and this year's figure can be agreed back to a quotation that the chief accountant was sent by the contractor. The audit senior has recorded evidence of this assessment within the current file as part of the firm's wider audit testing.	▼

Picklist

- Does not require to be adjusted
- Requires to be adjusted

Chapter summary

- Audit procedures exist for a variety of assertions depending on the area of the financial statements under review and again you will need to be able to produce written procedures as part of your assessment:
  - Non-current assets – capitalisation and relevant assertions including right-of-use asset leases
  - Inventory – the role of the inventory count, plus specific tests for different types of inventory (raw materials, work in progress or WIP and finished goods) and how to test for the correct treatment around the year end (cut-off)
  - Receivables – procedures are focused on circularisation (including the process itself and analysing the outcome of such a process)
  - Cash and bank – two key controls exist in this area (the bank letter and the bank reconciliation) so you need to be able to explain how each works
  - Borrowings – loans and other long-term liabilities
  - Payables – trade and others
  - Allowances – including depreciation, impairments to inventory and write-downs on doubtful debts
  - Revenue – using double entry to prove this amount by comparison with receivables
  - Payroll – again, using double entry to verify this amount as an expense in the statement of profit or loss
  - Purchases – includes any other expenses

Activity answers

Activity 1: JICS driving school

The correct answers are:

	✓
10 × Ford Fiestas	
2 × PCs and monitors for the office	
2 × desk telephones	
10 × mobile telephones	
Car insurance	✓
Car servicing	✓
Installation of dual controls in cars	
Replacement tyre for car no. 6	✓
Repairs to bumper of car no. 4	✓
Office fixtures and fittings	
'JICS' signs to go on top of cars	

There is logic that certain expenditure is capitalised when servicing (literally) a non-current asset. However, **tyres** and **repairs** are generally regarded as fair wear and tear, so in practice they are referred to as revenue items.

Insurance and **servicing** are also classified as ongoing operating costs.

There may be a *de minimis* level for non-current assets to be created in order to keep such records manageable, so items like **desk telephones** may fall beneath this threshold and be lost within normal operating costs, but they are kept as non-current assets here for consistency.

Activity 2: Campey Ltd non-current assets

Completeness

(1) Compare non-current assets balance on general ledger with non-current asset register and reconcile any differences.

(2) Select a sample of non-current assets from knowledge of the business and trace them to the non-current asset register.

(3) Review any sensitive items within the statement of profit or loss, such as motoring expenses and building repairs, to ensure that items which should have been capitalised throughout the year have not been expensed instead.

Rights and obligations

(1) Review title deeds for land and buildings to confirm ownership.

(2) Review vehicle registration documents for a sample of company vehicles to confirm ownership.

(3) Review lease documentation to establish any finance lease obligations regarding non-current assets.

Existence

(1) Select a sample of assets from the non-current asset register and physically trace them to those assets.

(2) Inspect the assets to ensure that they exist, are in good order and are obviously being used by Campey Ltd.

Accuracy, valuation and allocation

(1) As assets have not been revalued during the year, testing should start with additions. Confirm the amounts included at cost by reviewing the invoices for new vehicles and fittings.

(2) Recalculate the depreciation charge for a sample of assets.

(3) Review the bases for depreciation to ensure that 2% straight line for buildings, 25% diminishing balance for vehicles and 15% straight line for fittings are still reasonable.

(4) Use inspection evidence (from existence testing above) to confirm reasonableness of valuations for assets, especially impairments of land and buildings due to market conditions, dilapidation etc.

Activity 3: Paper Products Ltd

Often, the auditor has matters to consider before attending the inventory count in order to be prepared, matters to consider during the count itself and matters to consider after the count has taken place. The following is a summary of these three areas of consideration.

Before:

(1) Preparation

- (i) Review working papers from the previous year
- (ii) Determine arrangements with management in advance
- (iii) Become familiar with nature of inventory
- (iv) Consider need for an expert
- (v) Inventory held by/for third parties – review procedures to account for this
- (vi) Review client's count of physical inventory instructions. This should include the following:
    - (a) In writing
    - (b) Two independent counts
    - (c) Systematic clearing of areas
    - (d) Identification of obsolete damaged inventory
    - (e) Supervision
    - (f) Cut-off considered
    - (g) Count sheets - pre-numbered, written in ink and controlled in distribution and collection
    - (h) Investigation of differences – what happens if two counts disagree?

(2) Determine audit procedures required to cover a representative selection of inventory and inventory locations

(3) Identify potential problem/risk areas

During:

(1) Review client staff – are they following the instructions?

(2) Test counts, from the physical inventory to the records and vice versa

(3) Note damaged, old and obsolete inventory for valuation purposes

(4) Review WIP for stage of completion

(5) Inventory held by client for third parties must be excluded from count

(6) Take note of last goods received note (GRN) and goods despatch note (GDN)

(7) Form an overall impression of inventory levels/values

After:

(1) Check sequence of inventory sheets

(2) Check client's computation of final inventory figure

(3) Trace own test count items through to inventory sheets

(4) Check replies from third parties

(5) Inform management of general problems

(6) Follow up cut-off details

Activity 4: Inventory assertions

Test	Assertion
Test Form an opinion of the condition of inventory and record any instances of damage or obsolescence. **Result** There were 15 × 10m rolls of fabric stored near the roof of the warehouse where birds had nested, making the fabric unusable.	Accuracy, valuation and allocation
Test Trace 10 × 10m rolls of fabric from the inventory sheets to the relevant shelves of the warehouse. **Result** All 10 rolls were found on the shelves in the locations specified by the main accounting system.	Existence
Test Trace 10 × 10m rolls of fabric from the relevant shelves of the warehouse to the inventory sheets. **Result** All 10 rolls were traced back to the list generated by the main accounting system.	Completeness
Test Confirm that the fabric and garments held in the secure off-site storage facility are to be included in Glad Rags' inventory balance by verifying them to supporting documentation and invoices. **Result** All rolls of fabric and garments were traced back to storage invoices and haulage records, confirming that they belong to Glad Rags.	Rights and obligations

Activity 5: Valuing inventory

General

Cast the inventory listing to establish that it is mathematically correct.

Confirm that an appropriate basis of valuation (first in first out) is being used, through a discussion with management.

Compare the gross profit percentage to the previous year or industry data.

Cost

For a sample of products, vouch the purchase prices to suppliers' invoices to ensure cost is correctly recorded on the inventory listing.

NRV

For a sample of inventory items held at the year end, obtain NRV by reviewing the post year end sales price.

Where NRV is lower than cost, ensure the items are written down to NRV.

Confirm that inventories are included at lower of cost and NRV in the financial statements.

Activity 6: Hodgson Ltd

All three categories

- Record basis of valuation used in all three categories and ensure disclosure is accurate and inclusion in each category is appropriate
- Test material costs
  - Trace back to individual invoices
  - Ensure FIFO or appropriate bases being used
  - Review quantities used in WIP/finished goods
- Test labour costs
  - Trace calculations to supporting documentation (eg timesheets)
  - Review costing against actual labour and production statistics

WIP and **finished goods** only

- Ensure only production overheads are included (and that standard costs are still appropriate)
- Ensure based on normal activity levels

WIP only

- Review for reasonableness of assumptions – consider physical inspection
- Test calculations to ensure accurate

Finished goods only

- Follow through items noted at inventory count
- Review sales (volumes and prices) after year-end
- Review future orders to establish demand and likely sales prices
- Consider any background knowledge obtained during the audit
- Establish extent of any write-downs from past year
- Ensure any necessary adjustments to valuations have been made in light of this evidence (such as impairments to finished goods)

Activity 7: Cut-off testing

The correct answers are:

	No further action ✓	Refer to supervisor ✓
Revenues cut-off testing:	✓	
Purchases cut-off testing:		✓

Regardless of whether the order from Terry's Threads was a regular order that came early or late, it has to be accounted for consistently and, as such, if it has been accounted for as inventory received before the year end, there must be a matching purchase cost and payable balance at the year-end as well.

Activity 8: Circularisation

	Amount owed per sales ledger	Response from customer	Other information supplied by customer
British Clothes Stores plc	484,536	439,598	Cheque in post
IZK Ltd	74,973	74,973	n/a
Tisco Stores plc	78,805	71,663	Disputed invoice
J Club Ltd	323,024	323,024	n/a
Cavanaghs Ltd	14,388	nil	Goods not received yet
H and T Ltd	18,933	nil	Cheques in post
Nice Clothes Ltd	17,231	nil	Cheques in post
Ginger Ltd	22,315	22,315	n/a

Tisco is the only one where you cannot agree the balance yourself – those that agree (IZK, J Club and Ginger) need no further work, while British Clothes Stores, H and T and Nice Clothes have all paid their amounts owed and the only differences are due to timing (missing amounts have appeared in post year end cash receipts).

The warehouse records show that Cavanaghs' goods were despatched so they should be dealt with consistently, leaving the disputed invoice for Tisco. It is possible that their goods were not fully despatched or that some were damaged in transit – you need to perform more work on this before you can agree the balance as a valid trade receivable.

Activity 9: Pond Ltd

The following balances could be sampled:

	£
Wed-Me Ltd	(8,429)
Astra Stones Ltd	Nil
Jewels 'r' Us Ltd	3,294
Magnifique Ltd	987

Other than size, you would test for collectability and any other risks – **Astra** having a nil balance might be correct, but you need to confirm this. Jewels 'r' Us and Magnifique are both overdue so should be investigated (and used to assess the company's allowance for doubtful debts) while any credit balance on the sales ledger should be investigated further.

Activity 10: Bank reconciliation

(a) Audit procedures to be performed on the bank reconciliation:

Agree balance per cash book to cash book

Recalculate arithmetic

Agree balance per bank statement on the reconciliation back to bank statement

Agree balance per bank statement back to bank letter

Vouch unpresented cheques and outstanding lodgements to after-date bank statements

Agree bank error to after-date statements and supporting documentation

Review bank letter for any undisclosed accounts

(b) The correct answers are:

	✓
Bank error	
Items to be written off	✓
Arithmetic	
Disclosure items	
Errors with source data	✓

There are **two issues** that you may have spotted with this bank reconciliation – the **first** is that one of the outstanding cheques seems much older than the other two from their numbers, which might suggest a cheque that might never get presented and, as such, may require writing off the relevant accounts.

The **second** issue is that the bank reconciliation does not balance (£52,**296** vs £52,**926**). This could be due to a transposition error when producing the reconciliation or an error in the cash book or bank statement – both of which would need following up with the entity's staff.

Activity 11: HEC Ltd

The following work should be carried out on the loan:

- Obtain a schedule showing what is due in more than one year and what is due in less than one year
- Test the calculations to ensure that this analysis is correct, that interest has been treated correctly and that the total balance payable agrees to the bank letter
- Ensure that appropriate disclosure has been made in the financial statements

Activity 12: Gavilar Ltd

Objective	Suggested audit procedures
Completeness	Review trade payables using analytical procedures, comparing to previous year or budgets Review goods received notes around the year end to ensure purchases have been correctly treated for cut-off purposes Review unpaid invoice files for any liabilities not yet provided for Review after-date payments for any liabilities not recorded Obtain a list of trade payables and reconcile to the financial statements
Rights and obligations	Circularise trade payables (the procedure is similar to that used for trade receivables) Reconcile payables balances at the year end to a supplier's statement and follow up any discrepancies. Both these tests also provide evidence of completeness and accuracy, valuation and allocation
Accuracy, valuation and allocation	Ensure closing provisions/accruals are calculated in accordance with accounting policies and are consistent

Objective	Suggested audit procedures
Existence	Circularise trade payable and/or reconcile using suppliers' statements Perform cut-off tests on purchases and credit notes
Presentation	Ensure trade payables have been properly analysed between those due in less than one year and those due in more than one year

Other payables will include amounts due to be paid that do not form part of normal cost of sales (such as administration overheads, energy costs, rentals and insurance costs). In practice, they will not be treated any differently to trade payables but their patterns may be different, meaning that analytical procedures need to take this into account.

Activity 13: Adjustments

Matter	Adjust?
The auditor has found an invoice for office supplies ordered and delivered on the last day of the financial year. The invoice amount has not been included in the total for purchases in the statement of profit or loss. The amount for these supplies is material.	Requires to be adjusted
The auditor has completed analytical review of the cost of sales for a bakery. This analysis has indicated that ingredient costs per loaf have increased from 12.8 pence in the previous year to a figure closer to £3.56 per loaf. The non-financial information on the numbers of loaves has been corroborated during the audit.	Requires to be adjusted
The auditor has selected 20 payments from the purchase ledger total and has been tracing them back to invoices for evidence of both existence and valuation. Of these 20 payments, 19 have been traced successfully back for both assertions. The 20th item has no invoice and relates to health and safety assessments carried out at the entity's head office. A similar amount was included in last year's statement of profit or loss and this year's figure can be agreed back to a quotation that the chief accountant was sent by the contractor. The audit senior has recorded evidence of this assessment within the current file as part of the firm's wider audit testing.	Does not require to be adjusted

The third example is far from clear-cut without any materiality or risk assessments to refer to, but is an example of how the auditor looks for **corroborative evidence** that seems **plausible.** In this example, although we have no back-up for this payment, a matching quotation was issued and the amount is both ongoing and consistent with what the auditors understand of the entity; hence, both **valuation** and **existence** have some **persuasive evidence**, rather than being **conclusive**.

In such a case, it is probable that the weight of evidence is stacked in the entity's favour and the auditor's opinion (note – this is not a guarantee) is likely to be that the financial statements are free from material misstatement.

Test your learning

1 **Select whether the following statements are true or false.**

Statement	True or false?
Inventory is difficult to audit because it often consists of a large number of low value items which are collectively material.	▼
Key assertions to test in relation to inventory are existence, completeness and accuracy, valuation and allocation.	▼

Picklist

- False
- True

2 **Select whether the following statements are true or false.**

Statement	True or false?
It is important to record cut-off correctly so that assets are not double counted (receivables and inventory).	▼
It is important to record cut-off correctly so that a liability is not omitted in respect of an asset (payables and inventory).	▼
For the purposes of the financial statements, it does not matter if the company misstates cut-off between raw materials and work in progress.	▼

Picklist

- False
- True

3 The objective of a substantive procedure will determine the source of evidence obtained.

Required

For each of the objectives set out below, select the source of evidence.

Objective	Source of evidence
Obtain evidence of the value of raw material	▼
Obtain evidence of the value of finished goods	▼

Picklist

- Both
- Purchase invoice
- Sales invoice

4 **Complete the following statements about how net realisable value is tested.**

Net realisable value is tested with reference to after the year-end [▼].

The value of items of inventory is compared to post year-end [▼].

This is to ensure that inventory value is equal to or [▼] than net realisable value of the inventory.

Picklist

- Higher
- Lower
- Purchase invoices
- Purchases
- Sales
- Sales invoices

5 Auditors will carry out the following tests when auditing inventory.

Required

From the options provided, select which important assertion about inventory each test is seeking to prove in the first instance.

Test	Assertion
Attending an inventory count	▼
Tracing counted items to final inventory sheets	▼
Reviewing after year-end sales invoices	▼

Picklist

- Accuracy, valuation and allocation
- Completeness
- Existence

6 **Select which of the following statements best summarises the assertions the auditors are concerned with in respect of non-current assets by ticking the appropriate box.**

	✓
Auditors are concerned with completeness, existence, rights and obligations and accuracy, valuation and allocation.	
Auditors are concerned with completeness, existence and accuracy, valuation and allocation.	
Auditors are concerned with existence, accuracy, valuation and allocation and occurrence.	
Auditors are concerned with existence, accuracy, valuation and allocation, occurrence and accuracy.	

7 Auditors usually test receivables by carrying out a circularisation and/or review of receipts after the year end.

Required

Select which assertions the auditors are seeking evidence about.

Procedure	Assertion(s)
Receivables circularisation	▼
Reviewing sales receipts after year end	▼

Picklist

- Accuracy, valuation and allocation
- Both
- Rights and obligations

8 Select which of the following statements concerning the audit of revenue is incorrect by ticking the appropriate box.

	✓
Auditors usually rely 100% on controls over revenue by carrying out only controls testing.	
Auditors may test controls over revenue but will also carry out some substantive procedures, often restricted to analytical procedures as there is usually ample evidence concerning a company's revenue.	
Auditors will often only test revenue by analytical procedures as there is usually ample evidence concerning a company's revenue.	
Auditors will sometimes test completeness of revenue by tracing a sample of revenue from sales order to general ledger.	

9 State whether the following statements are true or false in respect of bank letter requests.

Statement	True or false?
Bank letter requests are sent out by the auditor directly to the bank.	▼
Bank letter requests should be made at the year-end date.	▼
Auditors will commonly test cash balances even if they are not material.	▼

Picklist

- False
- True

10 Select which of the following statements best summarises the issues that auditors are concerned with in respect of trade payables by ticking the appropriate box.

	✓
Auditors are concerned with completeness, existence and valuation.	
Auditors are concerned with completeness, existence and obligations.	
Auditors are concerned with existence, obligations and occurrence.	
Auditors are concerned with existence, obligations, occurrence and accuracy.	

11 State whether the following statements are true or false in respect of supplier statements.

Statement	True or false?
They represent a better source of evidence than replies to a receivables circularisation as they are sent direct to the company.	▼
They are only used when the auditor is unable to do a payables circularisation.	▼
Testing supplier statements provides evidence that trade payables have not been understated.	▼

Picklist

- False
- True

12 Complete the following statements about selecting a sample of trade payables:

Auditors should consider that payables might be [▼] and therefore not simply select large balances to test (although they must select [▼] items).

[▼] balances should also be incorporated into the test.

Picklist

- Material
- Nil
- Overstated
- Significant
- Understated

13 Select which of the following statements best summarises the issues that auditors are concerned with in respect of payroll expense by ticking the appropriate box.

	✓
Auditors are concerned with completeness, existence and valuation.	
Auditors are concerned with completeness, existence and obligations.	
Auditors are concerned with occurrence, accuracy and completeness.	
Auditors are concerned with existence, obligations, occurrence and accuracy.	

6 Reviewing and reporting findings

Learning outcomes

Having studied this chapter, you will be able to:

6	**Review and report findings**
6.1	**Matters to be referred to senior colleagues** Learners need to be able to: 6.1.1 assess misstatements for materiality 6.1.2 identify deviations from an organisation's prescribed procedures 6.1.3 identify matters: • unauthorised transactions • non-routine transactions • related party transactions • transactions above or below market rates • suspected fraud.
6.2	**Report audit findings** Learners need to understand: 6.2.1 elements of a report on deficiencies in internal control 6.2.2 that deficiencies in internal control are reported to: • management • the audit committee. Learners need to be able to: 6.2.3 identify the consequences of deficiencies in internal controls and how the deficiencies can be remedied 6.2.4 report findings.

Assessment context

This topic covers Task 9 in the assessment, so you should consider how to respond accordingly using the suggested activities.

Qualification context

As this is the final topic of this unit, there is an element of bringing the syllabus together so there will be plenty that you have seen before here. In order to report on your findings, you need to know how to communicate matters using appropriate terminology.

Business context

For many audit firms, evaluation is the most important element of the whole audit, where any outstanding issues are addressed prior to communicating the all-important opinion. For others, the audit opinion is merely the formality attached to the end of a process, necessary only to fulfil a legal obligation.

The audit profession in the 21st century is under enormous pressure to consider its future in the wake of ongoing financial reporting scandals: some outside observers feel that auditors should be subject to greater competition and regulation and be more responsible for the mistakes made by their clients, while others feel that putting too much pressure on the auditor will simply force many of them out of this line of work, leaving a skills and experience vacuum that could impact on quality and therefore increase the risk of mistakes being made by entities.

The key thing to remember here is that auditors need to review their findings and then report them appropriately.

Chapter overview

Reviewing and reporting findings

- Reporting matters to senior colleagues
  - Evaluation of matters identified during the audit for materiality and other issues
- Communicating deficiencies in internal control to those charged with governance and management
- The audit report and audit opinion

Introduction

Our audit journey is almost at an end and it has mirrored the audit process – having concluded that an audit is required, the audit has commenced.

We have reviewed systems of internal control and audit evidence as part of our understanding of how we would be able to deliver our audit opinion. We have then assessed the risks that stood in our way and considered the audit procedures that we would need to undertake in order to be in a position to reach that opinion.

Now we can complete the audit by evaluating all the evidence that we have collected and deciding on the most appropriate form of conclusion. This will require us to communicate our findings to different stakeholders in specific ways.

1 Reporting matters to senior colleagues

The overall completion process for the audit requires an amount of communication – in order to support the appropriate communication of the outcome of the audit, the auditor needs to ensure the following:

- All matters requiring further action have been addressed by the auditor
- All material and significant errors, deficiencies or other variations from standard are reported to those charged with governance and management (covered in the next section)
- The shareholders are given the most appropriate audit report that reflects the auditor's experience (covered in the final section of this chapter)

1.1 Evaluation of matters identified during the audit for materiality and other issues

It is almost inevitable that, during the course of the audit, a number of **misstatements** will be **uncovered**, some of them **material**, others clearly **trivial**. The auditor needs guidance to ensure that all such misstatements are both identified and recorded and that the most appropriate action is taken as a result.

The auditor must maintain a record of **all identified misstatements** (except those that are clearly trivial). As part of completion procedures, the auditor must evaluate the effect of these identified misstatements on the audit and the effect of uncorrected misstatements on the financial statements.

Auditing standards give guidance about this. The auditor must consider if the audit strategy and plan need revision if:

- The nature and circumstances of **identified misstatements** indicate that **other unidentified misstatements** exist, the combined total of which might be **material**.
- The **aggregate** of identified misstatements approaches the **materiality** level set by the auditors during planning

The auditors must **make management aware** of **identified misstatements** and request that they are adjusted. If they refuse, the auditors should take their reasons into account when evaluating if the financial statements as a whole are free from material misstatement.

Before assessing the effect that uncorrected misstatements have on the financial statements, the auditors should reconfirm that the **materiality level remains appropriate**. They should then determine whether the **aggregate** of the uncorrected misstatements is **material**.

The auditors should **communicate the uncorrected misstatements** to **those charged with governance** (listed individually). They should obtain a **written representation** from management and, where appropriate, from those charged with governance about whether they believe the uncorrected misstatements to be immaterial.

In addition to the list of uncorrected misstatements, the auditors should document the level below which items will be considered **trivial** and the auditor's conclusion as to whether uncorrected misstatements are material, and the reasons for that conclusion.

Besides **material misstatements**, the auditor is also required to evaluate any **deviations from an organisation's prescribed procedures.** This is likely to be connected to the work undertaken on the organisation's system of internal control where **control procedures** are either found to have **malfunctioned** or where **non-compliance** with a control has been identified (we will look at **deficiencies** identified in internal controls in the next section).

The following are **matters** that would need to be **identified** and **referred to senior colleagues** with some illustrative examples:

Matters	Examples
Unauthorised transactions	Purchases for which either no order was placed Acquisitions where there is no board minute approving the decision to proceed
Non-routine transactions	Disposals of non-current assets using practices or individuals that are inconsistent with policies (and which therefore may be indicative of fraud) Not following routine practices may lead to errors being made in accounting or other treatment
Related party transactions	Providing loans to directors at rates that may not be at arms-length Trading between companies with the same owners at rates that are not at arms-length
Transactions above or below market rates	Similar to above where there is a relationship that avoids normal arms-length prices Transfer prices for that are designed to artificially increase or decrease profits with a view to managing tax liabilities in certain jurisdictions
Suspected fraud	Excessive use of cash within a business may be an indication of money laundering Employees found in possession of inventory from the company's warehouse without a legitimate business need

Activity 1: Glad Rags

The audit junior is reviewing the audit documentation for the audit of Glad Rags and has requested your help in dealing with a number of issues that remain outstanding. Materiality is £100,000.

Required

In respect of each of these matters, select whether the audit junior should take no further action or refer it to their supervisor.

	No further action ✓	Refer to supervisor ✓
When reviewing the bank statements, the chief accountant removed some of the pages relating to the period of time after the year end.		
During his review of the payroll system, incorrect PAYE income tax rates were found to have been used. This was retrospectively corrected for the following month and all supporting transactions reviewed by the junior.		

	No further action ✓	Refer to supervisor ✓
Two outstanding balances within trade receivables are unlikely to be recoverable. One is for £55,000 and the other is £52,500. The financial accountant has concluded that as neither is above the materiality threshold used during the audit, the allowance for doubtful debts does not need to be adjusted for these balances.		
One of the company's premises has been disposed of using a different estate agent to the one that has always previously handled such transactions. In order to reflect the current market value, the carrying amount of the property is £325,000 but it was disposed of for £99,000. Despite the fact that no sales agreement was found, no further action has been recommended by the auditor as the disposal amount is below materiality.		
The sales director has been able to purchase goods for private use at 30% of retail price. This has been fully disclosed in a note to the financial statements.		

2 Communicating deficiencies in internal control to those charged with governance and management

In order to conclude their work, auditors are required to **report their findings**, including the communication of any deficiencies in internal control to **management** and **those charged with governance** (which could include an **audit committee** if one is required).

KEY TERM

Deficiency in internal control: When a control is designed, implemented or operated in such a way that it is unable to prevent, or detect and correct, misstatements in the financial statements on a timely basis, or a necessary control is missing.

This communication takes the form of a **report** which needs to be delivered in a **timely manner** and explain the following:

- The **main findings** from the audit, including **work done** and **conclusions drawn**
- Details of any **internal control deficiencies identified** during the course of the audit – this will include a **description** of each deficiency and a determination of whether they represent a **significant deficiency** (the auditor would not communicate all deficiencies, only those considered significant)
- The **consequences** of these deficiencies, meaning the auditor's **professional judgement** is required
- **Recommendations** for how these deficiencies can be **remedied**

Note. The process of communicating deficiencies, consequences and recommendations may vary between internal and external auditors – internal auditors would have a far broader remit, because external auditors are only required to report those deficiencies that they identified as a result of their statutory audit. However, there is no assurance provided by the auditor for this type of report as it is based on the facts that have emerged from the audit, so no opinion is necessary.

Activity 2: Reporting recommendations

Accounting system information – Glad Rags Revenue system

The company manufactures clothes to order from a catalogue. When an order is received, the sales department checks that the customer has not exceeded their credit limit and then issues a two-part order document. The sales department fills in the appropriate values for the order from current price lists. One copy is sent to the production department in order for the order to be completed and the other is filed alphabetically in the customer file in the sales department.

Once the order is completed, two-part despatch notes are raised. When the factory manager, Ian Jones, has checked the order, one copy of the despatch note is despatched with the goods (to be signed and returned), and one part is matched to the production department's sales order and sent to accounts to raise the invoice. Jane Hill raises the invoices from the order and despatch note, enters them on the computer and sends them out to customers.

Most customers pay in around 60 days. When they come in, cheques are passed to Beth Simpkins, one of the accounts assistants, and she updates the cash book and the sales ledger. Cheques are banked twice a week. Cheques are kept securely in the safe until banking.

Jane sends out statements to customers each month. Glad Rags' customers are mostly all reputable high street stores and there are rarely irrecoverable debts.

Required

Set out two deficiencies in the accounting systems for revenues at Glad Rags Limited as described above to be included in a report to those charged with governance. You should also set out the possible consequence of each deficiency and your recommendation for improvement.

3 The audit report and audit opinion

You already know that the primary objective of the audit is an expression of an opinion on the truth and fairness (or fair presentation) of the financial statements. The format of the auditor's report is laid down in the auditing standards as follows.

Summary of the content of an audit report with audit opinion

INDEPENDENT AUDITOR'S REPORT

To the shareholders of the company (or other appropriate addressee)

Opinion

(Includes the individual statements and the reporting period under review for the company being audited. It can use either 'give a true and fair view' or 'presents fairly, in all material respects' and states the relevant GAAP adopted.)

Basis for opinion

(This is always presented after the opinion and explains how the audit was conducted: the role of auditing and ethical standards as well as the audit evidence being sufficient and appropriate to provide a basis for the auditor's opinion.)

Material uncertainty relating to going concern

(Where applicable, the auditor shall report if there are any uncertainties that may cast significant doubt on the entity's ability to continue as a going concern.)

Key audit matters

(A list of the matters that were of the greatest significance from the audit; usually only required for listed entities.)

Other information

(This communicates whether there is anything to report regarding other information published within the annual report that contains the audited financial statements, eg a sustainability report.)

Responsibilities of management and those charged with governance for the financial statements

(Preparation and fair presentation of the financial statements, including internal controls, and the assessment of the company's ability to continue as a going concern.)

Auditor's responsibilities for the audit of the financial statements

(A detailed summary of the auditor's objectives, starting with obtaining reasonable assurance about the financial statements being free from material misstatements due to fraud or error.

Stresses the role of professional judgement and scepticism over accounting policies and estimates, judgements, internal controls, presentation, disclosure and communicating key audit matters and other issues with those charged with governance.)

Report on other legal and regulatory requirements

(Form and content of this section of the auditor's report will vary depending on the nature of the auditor's other reporting responsibilities.)

Signed

(Auditor's name and/or signature, address and date of the auditor's report)

Chapter summary

- Auditors need to be able to deal with any matters arising from the audit appropriately – this includes understanding what to do in certain situations including referral to senior colleagues:
  - Evaluating misstatements identified during the course of the audit for materiality
  - Identifying deviations from an organisation's prescribed procedures
  - Identifying other matters including transactions that are unauthorised, non-routine, related party transactions or above/below market rates, plus suspected fraud
- Communicating deficiencies in internal control to those charged with governance and management, including their consequences and recommendations on how to address them
- Formal communication to those stakeholders who use the financial statements is undertaken by issuing the auditor's report, which has a specific format and layout:
  - Title and addressee
  - An opinion and the basis for that opinion
  - Disclosures relating to material uncertainty relating to going concern, key audit matters and other information
  - Responsibilities of both auditors and management
  - Regulatory issues
  - Date and signature of the auditor

Activity answers

Activity 1: Glad Rags

The correct answers are:

	No further action ✓	Refer to supervisor ✓
When reviewing the bank statements, the chief accountant removed some of the pages relating to the period of time after the year end.		✓
During his review of the payroll system, incorrect PAYE income tax rates were found to have been used. This was retrospectively corrected for the following month and all supporting transactions reviewed by the junior.	✓	
Two outstanding balances within trade receivables are unlikely to be recoverable. One is for £55,000 and the other is £52,500. The financial accountant has concluded that as neither is above the materiality threshold used during the audit, the allowance for doubtful debts does not need to be adjusted for these balances.		✓
One of the company's premises has been disposed of using a different estate agent to the one that has always previously handled such transactions. In order to reflect the current market value, the carrying amount of the property is £325,000 but it was disposed of for £99,000. Despite the fact that no sales agreement was found, no further action has been recommended by the auditor as the disposal amount is below materiality.		✓
The sales director has been able to purchase goods for private use at 30% of retail price. This has been fully disclosed in a note to the financial statements.	✓	

The removal of some of the bank statements could be a sign that there are integrity issues with the chief accountant which the audit junior should pass on to the audit supervisor.

The retrospective correction means that this has been satisfactorily dealt with and requires no further work.

Although neither of the trade receivables balances is individually material, in aggregate they represent an amount that is material (£55,000 + £52,500 = £107,500) meaning that the failure to increase the allowance for these would represent a material misstatement. The supervisor should therefore be informed.

The property disposal represents a number of issues:

- It does not appear to have been authorised
- It is non-routine
- It has been conducted at below market rates
- The calculation of materiality is incorrect – the misstatement is actually £226,000 (the difference between the carrying amount of £325,000 and the disposal proceeds £99,000) which is material.

Consequently, the disposal should definitely be referred to the supervisor.

Although receiving a 70% discount is excessive, the fact that this related party transaction has been fully disclosed means that it has been treated in accordance with accounting standards, so no further action is required.

Activity 2: Reporting recommendations

Deficiency When invoices are raised, they are not reviewed to ensure that additions are correct.	**Deficiency** Post opening procedures appear unsupervised with no list of initial receipts – customer remittance information does not appear to be retained.
Consequence Invoices could be overstated (leading to loss of goodwill from customers) or understated (leading to a loss of funds for the company).	**Consequence** Receipts could be misappropriated or lost once at the company. Funds might not be effectively allocated against the correct customer, leading to incorrect records on outstanding amounts and irrecoverable debts.
Recommendation Invoices should be checked for additions prior to being sent out to customers for correct additions and VAT. This should be done by someone other than Jane (eg Beth) to introduce a second pair of eyes.	**Recommendation** A list of all receipts should be created on opening each item of post for completion purposes and all customer remittances retained and attached to cheques.

Test your learning

1 Here is a completed internal control questionnaire about controls in the wages system at MEM.

Internal control questionnaire: MEM wages system		
Question	**Y/N**	**Comment**
Are personnel records kept for each member of staff containing details of wage rates?	Yes	Kept in wages office
Does a senior member of staff authorise new employees and changes in rates of pay?	Yes	Authorised by Richard Bishop or Mark Bishop
Are any changes in pay rates recorded in the personnel records?	Yes	By personnel director, Cathy
Are hours worked recorded on timesheets/clocked?	Yes	Clock system in use
Is overtime approved by a senior member of staff?	Yes	Department heads review clock reports weekly
Are hours worked reviewed?	Yes	As above
Are wages reviewed against budget?	No	
Is a payroll prepared and approved before payment?	Yes	Prepared by Cathy, approved by Richard
Are total pay and deductions reconciled month on month?	Yes	
Where wages are paid in cash, is the wage cheque authorised?	N/A	
Is cash for wages payment kept securely?	N/A	
Is the identity of staff verified before cash payments are made?	N/A	
Are distributions of cash wages recorded?	N/A	
Are unclaimed wages kept securely?	N/A	
Where wages are paid by bank transfer, are transfer lists prepared and authorised?	Yes	Computer produces from payroll, Richard authorises
Are transfer lists compared to the payroll?	Yes	As above
Are details of deductions kept on employees' individual files?	Yes	
Are total pay and deductions reconciled month on month?	Yes	Computer highlights any discrepancies
Are costs of pay compared to budgets?	No	
Are gross pay and tax deducted per the payroll reconciled to returns made to the tax authorities?	Yes	Returns to tax office drafted from payroll by Cathy

Required

Identify the deficiency in the wages system at MEM and draft appropriate paragraphs to appear in a report to management concerning those control deficiencies, their consequences and suitable recommendations.

2 An audit client is in the middle of legal action with a former employee for sexual discrimination. If the employee wins the action, the company could have to pay compensation that would have a material impact on the financial statements.

Required

Set out the implications of this legal action for the auditors.

3 While performing final reviews on the audit file of a client, the auditor uncovers a series of outstanding matters.

Required

For each of the outstanding matters below, select whether the audit junior should take no further action or should refer to the supervisor.

Outstanding matter	Option
A company celebrated the 25th anniversary of its incorporation by organising a party for all of its staff, including those who were employed by the company 25 years ago. The costs associated with the party were processed differently to other costs associated with staff.	▼
During a review of the bank statements using a data analytics routine, a series of transactions has been identified where a sum of money has been received and then exactly 24 hours later, the same sum less 20% is paid out. There is no apparent business rationale for any of these transactions and their source and destination cannot be traced.	▼
From a sample of 100 credit sales accounts, 58 were found to have not followed company policy of performing a credit check before being set up. Credit sales for these accounts represent a material amount.	▼

Picklist

- No further action
- Refer to supervisor

4 During the audit of Zhong Ltd, the following deficiencies in general computer controls were discovered:

- No passwords are required to access any part of the computerised accounting system.
- While security backup copies of files are taken, these copies are kept in the desk occupied by the accounts clerk.

Required

Prepare extracts, suitable for inclusion in a report to management of Zhong Ltd, which set out the possible consequences of these deficiencies, and recommendations you would make in respect of them.

5 You are the external auditor of Festival Ltd, which is a bank operating in one developed country. During your testing of the bank's payroll and human resources (HR) systems, you discovered a number of issues:

- There are no system procedures for processing new starters and leavers on the payroll.
- The HR department has experienced staffing issues which has led to payroll staff helping out with some HR duties.
- Filing within the payroll department is behind schedule and a significant number of employee records are still being processed by the HR department, despite the relevant employees having either started or left the company.
- The payroll system has been computerised during the year of audit but, due to staff shortages, was not fully tested before being implemented.
- Staff have been booked onto training courses to keep up to date with accounting for tax and other statutory deductions, but due to workload pressures, they have not been able to attend these courses.

Required

Prepare extracts, suitable for inclusion in a report to management of Festival Ltd, which set out the following in respect of the matters described above:

- **The possible consequences, and**
- **The recommendations you would make.**

6 Jump is a leisure facility operated by a local government council on the outskirts of a large rural town. It has a swimming pool which offers lessons for children and adults as well as being open to the general public for recreational swimming. It has a gym with various fitness machines which members of the public can use either by paying a monthly subscription or on a pay-as-you-go basis. It also runs dance and fitness classes and has a cafeteria which serves food and drink. It is managed by the Head of Leisure Services who is based at the local council office in the town centre.

There is a car park at Jump that charges for parking due to its proximity to the local railway station. However, Jump does not employ any wardens to monitor parking. Cash is collected from parking machines and other tills and then returned to the general office for counting by gym instructors when they are not participating in a class. Subscriptions are also set up by gym instructors when they meet new members on their induction to the gym. Swimming lessons are paid for by direct transfers to Jump's bank account and amounts paid are reconciled by the Head of Swimming Lessons at the end of each month.

Maintenance of the fitness machines is carried out by gym instructors using information found online. The swimming pool is maintained by a retired engineer who comes in twice a week and over the weekends to monitor water purity and water usage statistics.

Accidents are logged in an accident book that requires the person's name, the date and time of their accident and any medical help administered.

Required

Prepare extracts, suitable for inclusion in a report to management of Jump, which set out the following in respect of the matters described above:

- **The possible consequences, and**
- **The recommendations you would make.**

Test your learning answers

Chapter 1

1 Internal control is the process designed , implemented and maintained by those charged with governance , management and other personnel to provide reasonable assurance about the achievement of the entity's objectives with regard to the reliability of financial reporting , effectiveness and efficiency of operations and compliance with applicable laws and regulations.

2

Activity	Type
A company should only pay for work done by employees.	Control objective
Company vehicles are used by employees for their own purposes.	Risk
Part C39t99, in regular use in the business, is reordered when inventory levels fall below 200.	Control procedure

3 The correct answer is:

	✓
Control activities will be similar in all sizes of company over core activities.	
A large company is likely to have a more formal control system than a small company.	
A small company is likely to have a less complex information system than a big company.	
A large company is more likely to have a good control environment than a small company.	✓

Control environment depends on the attitudes, awareness and actions of directors. Although some small companies may have difficulties in activating controls such as segregation of duties due to staff restrictions, the attitudes of management will not necessarily be poorer just because the company is small.

In practice, control activities will be similar in all sizes of company over core activities, although all companies differ and have some varying objectives, so controls will alter from company to company to some extent. Large and small companies are likely to be different in terms of the formality of their control environment, or the formality and extent of their information systems.

4 Control objectives over wages:

(1) Employees only paid for work done

(2) Gross pay calculated correctly and authorised

(3) Gross pay, net pay and deductions correctly recorded on payroll

(4) Wages and salaries paid recorded properly in bank records

(5) Wages and salaries recorded correctly in the general ledger

(6) Deductions calculated correctly and authorised

(7) The correct amounts paid to the taxation authorities

5

Internal control procedure	Control objective
The payroll should be reconciled to other records, such as the cash payment for net pay per the bank's records.	Gross pay, net pay and deductions should be correctly recorded on payroll.
The payroll should be authorised by someone other than the personnel director.	Gross pay should be calculated correctly and authorised.

6

Internal control procedure	Risk mitigated
Non-current assets are inspected regularly.	Assets are not maintained properly for use in the business.
Capital expenditure is approved by the purchasing director on behalf of the board.	Assets are bought from inappropriate suppliers at inflated cost.

7

Internal control procedure	Risk mitigated
Inventory store is kept locked.	Inventory is stolen.
Goods inwards are checked for quality.	Damaged inventory is valued in the financial statements.

8

Action	Type of control activity
Person A matches dispatch notes to invoices; Person B creates invoice to customer	Segregation of duties
Control account reconciliation	Arithmetic and accounting control
Petty cash box kept locked	Physical control
Adequate resourcing of accounting function	Organisational control
Review of budgetary control report	Management control

9

Activities	Type of security control
Validation of input data	Integrity control
Passwords	Physical access control
Encryption	Logical control
Archiving	System control

10 Management should regularly ensure that staff perform [reconciliations] of the receivables ledger to ensure accuracy and completeness of the data.

11 Control objectives in relation to taking orders and extending credit are part of the [sales] system of the accounting system.

12 Completion of GRNs is a control activity related to the control objective of [only accepting goods and services that have been ordered and appropriately authorised].

13 Allocating one customer's payment to another customer's account in order to balance the books and detract from a shortfall is called [teeming and lading].

14

Situation	Fraud triangle condition
'They never check on the older items in the warehouse, so they are the easiest ones to steal.'	Opportunity
'I have worked so hard for this company over the years and yet no-one notices. I am definitely entitled to take items out of the stationery cupboard for my own personal use.'	Rationalisation
'If I don't find the money in the next week, my house will be repossessed by the building society. I have to steal cash from the safe because I have no other way of finding the money I owe.'	Pressure

15

Activities	Type of security control
Batch processing of invoices	Completeness
Only the finance manager can authorise new suppliers on the system	Segregation of duties
Sequential numbering of invoices	Integrity
Alerts to the user when the journal being entered does not balance	Integrity

16 The correct answers are:

	✓
Cost effectiveness	✓
Ease of use	
Reliable	✓
Providing timely information	✓

Ease of use is not a specific objective of an accounting system although it is fair to say that this would be a desirable feature. The accounting system should meet the requirements of the organisation in providing reliable and timely information in a cost-effective manner.

17 The correct answers are:

	✓
Time	
Responsibility	
Likelihood	✓
Volatility	
Impact	✓

18 The correct answers are:

	✓
Morale	✓
Social	
Reputation	✓
Environmental	
Financial	✓

19 The correct answer is:

	✓
During the analysis of the sales system, a fraud matrix graded the potential loss from misappropriation to be rated 5. Management have decided urgent action is required.	✓
A fraud matrix is a subjective analysis of an organisation's controls, and will ensure that all recommendations identified are actioned immediately.	
A control within the payroll system has been rated as 2 within the fraud matrix. Management have decided that this risk must be rectified immediately.	

A fraud matrix enables the prioritisation of the key risks, focusing on the most significant first. An organisation will then deal with the highest risks first, which is why a fraud matrix grades the risks rather than dealing with all of the weaknesses at the same time.

A fraud matrix rates the lowest risk as 1 and the highest as 5, therefore anything rated 5 should be prioritised over lower rated risks.

Chapter 2

1 The correct answer is:

	✓
It is seen as distinct from its owners.	
It is required to have an audit, unless exempt.	
It must keep accounting records.	
It must be managed by its owners.	✓

A company does not have to be managed by its owners. However, registering a company does mean that it is seen as a separate entity from its owners, and that it must satisfy certain requirements of the Companies Act, such as keeping accounting records and having its financial statements audited.

2 A(n) [audit] is an exercise carried out by [auditors] to ascertain whether the [financial statements] prepared by the [directors] are (in the UK) in accordance with UK GAAP and the [Companies Act 2006] and give what is known as a(n) [true and fair view] .

3

Statement	True or false?
Auditors are required to report on the truth and fairness of financial statements.	True
Auditors have a right of access to a company's books and records at any time.	True
Auditors are entitled to obtain explanations from the officers of a company.	True

4 The correct answer is:

	✓
All users of financial statements	
The client (that is, the company, comprising all the shareholders)	
Shareholders	
The client and any other parties with whom they have implied a special relationship	✓

5 (i) A **duty of care** existed, it was (ii) **breached**, causing (iii) **loss**.

6 The correct answers are:

	✓
Company A is a small company that is unlisted but has voluntarily chosen to introduce an audit committee of two non-executive directors	✓
Company B is a listed entity which has an audit committee consisting of four non-executive directors where recent and relevant financial experience is provided by the finance director	
Company C is a small company that is also a bank so has opted not to have an audit committee	
Company D is a listed entity that has an audit committee consisting of three non-executive directors	✓

As a small company, Company A can operate an audit committee that has only two non-executive directors.

Company B has satisfied all of the requirements of the Code apart from the role played by the finance director, who is precluded from being appointed due to being an executive director (and would in effect be responsible for reviewing their own work if they sat on the audit committee).

Company C is not a straightforward situation, but banks are not allowed to be designated as small companies so this seems unlikely; Company D however satisfies all the criteria from the Code, making it the best available option after Company A.

7 The correct answers are:

	✓
Apply	
Explain	✓
Comply	✓
Report	

The principle used by the UK Corporate Governance Code is called 'comply or explain'.

8 The correct answer is:

	✓
The board of directors	
HMRC	
The audit firm's money laundering reporting officer	✓
All of the above	

9 The correct answer is:

	✓
Controls are always monitored by an internal audit function, as this is the purpose of their existence.	
Controls are monitored by the directors of a company.	
Controls are monitored by the people who operate them, as they are in the best position to assess whether the objectives of the controls are being met.	
Who monitors controls depends on the size of the company and its personnel: it may be an internal audit function, but it could also be the directors, or department heads.	✓

Who monitors controls will vary from company to company. Larger companies may have internal audit functions, one of whose key purposes will be to monitor controls. In small companies, control monitoring is less likely to be formal and is likely to be carried out by the staff in charge of each function or department.

Chapter 3

1 The correct answer is:

	✓
In order to understand internal control systems	
In order to be able to assess risks	✓
In order to see what items there are to be audited	
In order to eliminate items from testing	

This will then direct auditors as to what to test and how.

2 [Audit] risk is the risk that the auditors give an [inappropriate] opinion on the financial statements.

[Control] risk is the risk that the entity's internal control system will not prevent or detect and correct errors.

[Inherent] risk is the risk that items will be misstated due to their [nature] or due to their [context].

[Detection] risk is the risk that misstatements will exist in financial statements and the auditors will not discover them.

3

Statement	True or false?
Auditors cannot affect inherent and control risk as inherent and control risks are the risks that errors will arise in the financial statements as a result of control problems or the nature of items in the financial statements of the entity. The auditors cannot control those factors.	True
If inherent and control risk are high, detection risk should be rendered low to come to an overall acceptable level of risk. In order for detection risk to be low, the auditors will have to carry out a low level of testing.	False

Detection risk should be low, but to achieve that auditors should carry out a high level of testing.

4

Factor	Impact?
The control environment is weak and there is considerable pressure on management to improve results year on year.	Increase
Management has implemented improvements in controls as a result of weaknesses identified last year.	Reduce

5

Statement	True or false?
Materiality is the concept of significance to users of the financial statements.	True
'Material and pervasive' in relation to disclosures means anything related to directors.	False

Material and pervasive disclosures are those that are fundamental to users' understanding of the financial statements.

6

The company has diversified its operations during the year.	Increase
The company has discontinued operations in its riskiest operating area during the year.	Increase

Although discontinuing operations might seem as though it would reduce risk, in this year, the company will have to meet accounting requirements relating to the changes, which increases audit risk.

Chapter 4

1

Assertion	Category
Existence	Account balances
Accuracy, valuation and allocation	Account balances
Cut-off	Classes of transaction

2 The correct answer is:

	✓
All sampling units should have an equal chance of being selected for testing.	✓
All audit areas must be subject to sampling.	
Auditors must always stratify a population to focus attention on high value items.	
The more items there are in a population, the higher the sample sizes must be.	

The other statements are all untrue.

3

Instance	Method
Simran has been asked to select a sample of 12 sales invoices to trace from sales order to general ledger. There are 16 folders of sales orders for the year, stored in the sales office.	Haphazard
Julie has been asked to select a sample of 5 purchase ledger accounts to carry out a supplier statement reconciliation. There are 16 purchase ledger accounts.	Systematic
Ben is selecting a sample of inventory lines to perform a valuation test. The audit team have been instructed to use the computerised techniques available to them, one of which is a sample selection program.	Random

Where there is such a large population, Simran should select on a haphazard basis.

However, where there is a small population, ordered in a way that does not bias the sample (for example, alphabetically), systematic selection is suitable for Julie.

If a computerised random numbers program is available, it could be used by Ben as a suitable method of selecting a non-biased sample.

4

Matters	Impact
Increase in the auditor's assessment of the risk of material misstatement	Increase
Increase in tolerable misstatement	Decrease
Decision to stratify a large population	Decrease

5 Automated tools and techniques are methods of obtaining [evidence] by using [computers]. [Audit software] is [software] that can check [data] on computer systems by [interrogating] or by comparing versions of [programs]. [Test data] is a way of checking computer [programming] by inputting real or false information and observing how the program deals with it.

Chapter 5

1

Statement	True or false?
Inventory is difficult to audit because it often consists of a large number of low value items which are collectively material.	True
Key assertions to test in relation to inventory are existence, completeness and accuracy, valuation and allocation.	True

2

Statement	True or false?
It is important to record cut-off correctly so that assets are not double counted (receivables and inventory).	True
It is important to record cut-off correctly so that a liability is not omitted in respect of an asset (payables and inventory).	True
For the purposes of the financial statements, it does not matter if the company misstates cut-off between raw materials and work in progress.	False

3

Objective	Source of evidence
Obtain evidence of the value of raw material	Purchase invoice
Obtain evidence of the value of finished goods	Both

Finished goods will be tested for purchase price, cost of conversion (so purchase documentation) and also net realisable value (hence also testing after-date sales invoices)

4 Net realisable value is tested with reference to after the year-end [sales].

The value of items of inventory is compared to post year-end [sales invoices].

This is to ensure that inventory value is equal to or [lower] than net realisable value of the inventory.

5

Test	Assertion
Attending an inventory count	Existence
Tracing counted items to final inventory sheets	Completeness
Reviewing after year-end sales invoices	Accuracy, valuation and allocation

6 The correct answer is:

	✓
Auditors are concerned with completeness, existence, rights and obligations and accuracy, valuation and allocation.	✓
Auditors are concerned with completeness, existence and accuracy, valuation and allocation.	
Auditors are concerned with existence, accuracy, valuation and allocation and occurrence.	
Auditors are concerned with existence, accuracy, valuation and allocation, occurrence and accuracy.	

7

Procedure	Assertion(s)
Receivables circularisation	Rights and obligations
Reviewing sales receipts after year end	Both

Receivables circularisation may result in a customer confirming that the debt exists (in other words, rights and obligations) but if they are unable to pay it, evidence of the debt's valuation has not been obtained.

Looking at receipts after-date confirms valuation and that the company was owed that debt in the first place.

8 The correct answer is:

	✓
Auditors usually rely 100% on controls over revenue by carrying out only controls testing.	✓
Auditors may test controls over revenue but will also carry out some substantive procedures, often restricted to analytical procedures as there is usually ample evidence concerning a company's revenue.	
Auditors will often only test revenue by analytical procedures as there is usually ample evidence concerning a company's revenue.	
Auditors will sometimes test completeness of revenue by tracing a sample of revenue from sales order to general ledger.	

This is incorrect as revenue is almost certainly a material balance, which must be subject to some detailed testing (which may be analytical procedures only or tests of detail or a combination). Auditors may choose not to test controls at all if they appear weak.

9

Statement	True or false?
Bank letter requests are sent out by the auditor directly to the bank.	True
Bank letter requests should be made at the year-end date.	False
Auditors will commonly test cash balances even if they are not material.	True

Bank letter requests are sent out by the auditor directly to the bank (although the bank will only reply if the client has given them permission to).

Bank letter requests should be made about a month in advance of the year end to allow the bank time to process it.

Auditors will commonly test cash balances even if they are not material because cash is highly susceptible to fraud.

10 The correct answer is:

	✓
Auditors are concerned with completeness, existence and valuation.	
Auditors are concerned with completeness, existence and obligations.	✓
Auditors are concerned with existence, obligations and occurrence.	
Auditors are concerned with existence, obligations, occurrence and accuracy.	

11

Statement	True or false?
They represent a better source of evidence than replies to a receivables circularisation as they are sent direct to the company.	False
They are only used when the auditor is unable to do a payables circularisation.	False
Testing supplier statements provides evidence that trade payables have not been understated.	True

Sending supplier statements direct to the company reduces their value as they could potentially be tampered with (however, they do still represent a good source of third-party evidence).

An auditor would only carry out a payables circularisation in exceptional circumstances.

12 Auditors should consider that payables might be [understated] and therefore not simply select large balances to test (although they must select [material] items). [Nil] balances should also be incorporated into the test.

13 The correct answer is:

	✓
Auditors are concerned with completeness, existence and valuation.	
Auditors are concerned with completeness, existence and obligations.	
Auditors are concerned with occurrence, accuracy and completeness.	✓
Auditors are concerned with existence, obligations, occurrence and accuracy.	

Chapter 6

1 **Deficiency: Failure to compare actual payroll costs to budget**

No one compares the cost of the payroll (wages, salaries, costs of employers' NI, any company pension contributions) to the budgeted cost at the start of the year.

Consequence

Errors may arise in the payroll (which could be highlighted by such comparison) and not be corrected which might result in overpayment of wages or of tax.

Recommendation

The payroll costs should be compared to budget on a monthly basis and variances investigated. The review should probably be carried out by Richard Bishop when he approves the payroll, although variance investigation could be carried out by someone else. This person should be someone other than Cathy to restrict opportunity for payroll fraud.

2 This would need to be referred to a senior colleague to consider the implications of the litigation on the financial statements regarding the following:

- Potential provision or disclosure required for the compensation
- Potential impact on going concern if the litigation gives ground for further claims

3

Outstanding matter	Option
A company celebrated the 25th anniversary of its incorporation by organising a party for all of its staff, including those who were employed by the company 25 years ago. The costs associated with the party were processed differently to other costs associated with staff.	No further action
During a review of the bank statements using a data analytics routine, a series of transactions has been identified where a sum of money has been received and then exactly 24 hours later, the same sum less 20% is paid out. There is no apparent business rationale for any of these transactions and their source and destination cannot be traced.	Refer to supervisor
From a sample of 100 credit sales accounts, 58 were found to have not followed company policy of performing a credit check before being set up. Credit sales for these accounts represent a material amount.	Refer to supervisor

For the 25th anniversary party, although this is a non-routine transaction, it is for an unusual event, so there is probably no precedent for it and as such, it is unlikely to be a matter requiring further consideration.

The cash sums appear to be a case of money laundering where the 20% could be a handling fee for the dealing with the proceeds of crime. If this is money laundering, care would need to be taken in the referral in order to avoid tipping off.

The failure to apply credit checks appears to have led to a possible overstatement of revenue if credit sales are unrecoverable. This should therefore be escalated to the supervisor.

4 **Consequences**

- Unrestricted access to the computer system could lead to error, deliberate alteration of accounting records, inefficiency and possible fraud.
- Files may be lost, damaged or accessed without authorisation.

Recommendations

- Your present software includes the facility to allow restricted access to systems by your staff through a structured system of passwords that can be changed frequently.

  We recommend that passwords should be introduced as soon as possible.
- We recommend that backup files are stored securely, for example, in a fire-proof safe.

5 **Possible consequences:**

(1) Without adequate procedures for dealing with starters and leavers, there is a risk that staff may be paid incorrectly once they have started or that leavers may continue to be paid after they have left (new starters who are underpaid are most likely to complain, so overpayments are the biggest risk here).

(2) Staffing issues could lead to fraud and/or error in the processing of payroll information (this is exacerbated by the lack of segregation of duties presented by the same staff performing both HR and payroll activities without supervision and review).

(3) As above, fraud and/or error could occur due to this lack of internal control. In addition, failure to safeguard employee's confidential details could lead to sanctions if the company fails to comply with data protection legislation.

(4) The new computerised system may include processing errors that have not yet been spotted, which could lead to problems with record-keeping and potential overpayments, as well as errors in the transfer of data.

(5) It is possible that statutory deductions (such as tax and national insurance) have not been made correctly, leading to possible misstatement of relevant amounts in the financial statements and potential fines from the tax authorities.

Recommendations:

(1) A suitable independent resource (such as internal audit if they exist) should perform an analysis of starters and leavers (such as tracing the first and last payment made to each one) going back over recent months to determine whether any overpayments have occurred and then attempt to quantify any misstatements.

(2) A selection of payroll records should be reviewed for compliance with policy and procedure (if any exist) and the extent of any fraud and/or error quantified (in the short term, this should again be completed by internal audit to maintain independence). Moving forward, staffing levels in both HR and payroll should be reviewed as a priority.

(3) As above, a review of record-keeping should be completed as a priority and the extent of any breaches in legislation should be established.

(4) A post-implementation review should be undertaken as a priority to establish whether there are any misstatements in the payroll and whether the system is operating as intended (staff may require training in the new system so human error should be considered as well).

(5) A reconciliation of deductions made compared to deductions due should be completed by internal audit to determine the extent of any misstatement and necessary training of payroll staff should be arranged as soon as possible.

6 Possible consequences:

(1) The absence of onsite management could lead to poor practices being adopted by staff at Jump.

(2) Without employing parking wardens, Jump could be missing out on revenue due from parking.

(3) Cash collection appears to lack segregation of duties and could be subject to either fraud or error due to inadequate numbers of staff performing this activity (the amounts of cash handled by Jump could be significant too, making this a significant risk).

(4) Maintenance of the gym equipment and swimming pool is not carried out by qualified staff, leading to the risk of negligence if the public use faulty equipment and are injured as a result.

(5) It is possible that Jump's pool is using more water than it should and that levels of chemicals used in the water may be inappropriate for general use and may not comply with health and safety regulations.

(6) The accident book process does not seem to differentiate between staff and users of the leisure facilities, and causes are not listed, meaning that any necessary action may not be properly identified.

Recommendations:

(1) The Head of Leisure Services should consider managing Jump from onsite.

(2) Wardens (or similar) should be costed up and employed if cost-effective.

(3) Cash collection staff should be costed up and employed if cost-effective.

(4) The adequacy of the current Fidelity Guarantee Insurance cover should be assessed by comparison to the amounts of cash handled regularly.

(5) Existing staff should be trained or specialist staff recruited to maintain all equipment at Jump.

(6) Specialist pool management knowledge should be provided to staff (see above) via training.

(7) More details should be recorded in the accident book ie staff/public; cause of accident; and need for remedial work at Jump etc.

Glossary

Chapter 1: Internal controls and fraud

Accounting controls: Controls which help to identify mistakes in the accounting records.

Authorisation and approval of transactions: Undertaken by supervisors and managers – this shows the person processing the transaction that it is valid, eg overtime should be approved by departmental heads.

Authorisation controls: These ensure that only authorised personnel can make changes, such as to standing data or to authorise a bank payment.

Control activities: Policies and procedures that help ensure that objectives are carried out.

Control environment: Formed by the attitudes, awareness and actions of management and those responsible for ensuring that the internal controls within the company meet that company's needs.

Control objectives: What a system is trying to do.

Control procedures: How a system achieves objectives and manages risks.

Fraud controls: Internal controls specifically against fraud in the areas of staff controls, management controls, physical controls and IT controls.

Fraud matrix: A map of the potential frauds against an organisation, cross-referenced to the risks of each of these occurring, documenting the controls over these risks. Also known as a risk matrix.

Fraud: A deliberate or intentional attempt to gain advantage by some form of deception.

Information processing controls: Controls relating to the transactions and standing data in the computerised accounting system.

Integrity controls: Controls that verify and validate input data, the processing of data and the production of reports.

Integrity of data: Ensures that data is complete, secure and accurate.

Internal controls: Policies and procedures that address the risk that the aims and objectives of the company will not be met.

Logical controls: Controls related to preventing unauthorised access to data within a system.

Misappropriation of assets: Theft, teeming and lading, payment of false employees or suppliers.

Misstatement of the financial statements: The overstatement of assets or profit, or the understatement of profit, losses or liabilities.

Monitoring, review and report: In this context, **monitoring** means looking at activity or behaviour related to a specified fraud risk because you need to know the extent of this activity or behaviour.

Review means gathering evidence of this activity or behaviour to understand the extent of this fraud risk.

Report means what you communicate to those higher up in the organisation as part of the overall risk management process.

Physical controls: Ensuring assets such as inventory and cash are safe by means of locked rooms and containers, cameras and security staff.

Processing controls: May be used to warn the user if they try to log out before processing is finished or close a document prior to saving. Data is also reviewed for arithmetical accuracy.

Reconciliations: Controls where staff ensure that two different sources of information agree or that any differences are understood, eg bank reconciliations verifying the bank statement to the bank account on the nominal ledger.

Reviews: Performed by supervisors or managers by looking at summaries and reports of transactions, eg to ensure they are reasonable.

Risks: What a system is trying to avoid.

Security controls: Controls in the accounting system that cover integrity controls, system controls and physical access controls.

Segregation of duties: Making sure that more than one person is involved in different parts of each process to minimise the opportunity for fraud and error.

System of internal control: The control environment, the entity's risk assessment process, the entity's processes to monitor the system of internal control, the information system and communication and control activities.

Systemic weaknesses: Weaknesses that arise within the accounting system itself, which leave it open to fraud and error.

Verification: The process of confirming that something is what it claims to be; in other words, that something can be said to be true. In accounting terms, this would include confirming an amount, date, name, location or event.

Chapter 2: The audit and assurance framework

Assurance: Assurance is a degree of confidence that is provided by a practitioner when reviewing subject matter produced by a responsible party for the benefit of the intended users of that subject matter. Assurance can be expressed in different ways and to different extents.

Audit committee: A collection of non-executive directors charged with overseeing various controls in place over the audited financial statements.

Audit failure: Performing a poor-quality audit resulting in the auditors being found guilty of negligence can be described as audit failure, which can have serious consequences for audit firms.

Audit, Risk and Governance Authority (ARGA): This body is expected to replace the FRC and will have more wide-ranging powers following a series of recent regulatory reforms in the UK. The creation of ARGA was included in the King's Speech to Parliament in 2024 but no further details have been issued by the Government, so for the purposes of your assessment, you can assume that the relevant standard-setting body in the UK is the FRC.

Audit: An audit is an independent review of the financial statements and disclosures produced by directors to ensure that they are both true and fair.

Complete: All information necessary for understanding the phenomenon being depicted is present.

Comply or explain: A company can either comply with the requirements of the Code, or they must explain how and why they have not complied, which provides flexibility and supports a more informed judgement for anyone relying on the audited financial statements.

Corporate governance: The system by which companies are directed and controlled (FRC, 2024).

Expectation gap: This term is used to describe the difference between the expectations of those who rely upon an auditor's report concerning the audit work they think should be performed and the actual work performed by the auditor.

Faithful representation: Financial information represents the economic substance rather than the legal form, possessing the characteristics of completeness, neutrality and being free from error.

Financial Reporting Council (FRC): The independent regulator of the accounting and auditing professions in the UK. The Government has delegated responsibility for standard setting to the FRC as well as quality inspections, corporate governance and disciplinary action across the accountancy profession.

Free from error: Processes and descriptions are without error. This does not mean perfectly accurate in all respects. It just explains any issues that might affect accuracy, such as the need to present an accounting estimate of some kind.

Internal audit: An independent control designed to evaluate and improve the effectiveness of governance, risk management and control processes in an organisation.

International Audit and Assurance Standards Board (IAASB): This is an independent body, part of the **International Foundation for Ethics and Audit (IFEA)**, which sets international standards on auditing that apply across multiple jurisdictions.

International Sustainability Standards Board (ISSB): The ISSB is responsible for developing international sustainability standards that will result in a high-quality, comprehensive global baseline of sustainability disclosures focused on the needs of investors and the financial markets.

The ISSB supports the creation of globally comparable information on sustainability-related risks and opportunities for the purposes of investment decision-making.

Note. While the information produced using ISSB standards may be useful to auditors, these standards are not relevant to an audit of financial statements.

Liability limitation agreement: An agreement between an auditor and their client that limits the amount of auditor liability in the event of any negligence.

Negligence: The way in which a service is carried out (ie carelessly) and the legal wrong which arises when a person breaks a legal duty of care that is owed to another and causes loss to that other.

Neutral: Without bias, supported by the exercise of prudence (prudence is the exercise of caution when making judgements under conditions of uncertainty).

Non-executive director: A board member whose responsibility it is to evaluate the effectiveness of the financial reporting process.

Professional scepticism: An attitude that includes a questioning mind, being alert to conditions which may indicate possible misstatement due to error or fraud, and a critical assessment of evidence. Auditors should be prepared to challenge such conditions as required.

Proportional liability: Where a professional firm agrees to be liable for only a share of any damages due to a client on respect of negligence or other litigation.

Those charged with governance: The directors of a company who are responsible for managing the company on behalf of the shareholders.

True and fair view: 'True' means honest and factual, while 'fair' means unbiased and free from discrimination.

Chapter 3: Planning and risk assessment

Audit risk: The risk that the auditor does not detect one or more of the risks that relate to an audit and gives an opinion that the financial statements are true and fair when, in reality, they are materially misstated in some way due to incorrect and/or inappropriate accounting or disclosure. It is a factor of inherent risk, control risk and detection risk.

Control risk: The risk that a misstatement that could occur in a transaction, account balance or disclosure and that could be material, either individually or when aggregated with other misstatements, will not be prevented, or detected and corrected, by the entity's internal control. Auditors therefore need to understand the controls in place within an entity as a way of addressing inherent risk.

Detection risk: Detection risk is the risk that audit procedures will not detect a misstatement. It is a representation of the acceptable amount of risk faced by the auditor. As inherent and control risk increase, the level of acceptable detection risk decreases and the auditor therefore performs more testing to keep audit risk at an acceptable level.

Inherent risk: The susceptibility of a transaction, account balance or disclosure to a misstatement that could be material, either individually or when aggregated with other misstatements, before consideration of any related controls. Examples of inherent risk factors include complexity, subjectivity, change, uncertainty and the risk of management bias or fraud.

Material and pervasive:

- Are not confined to specific elements, accounts or items of the financial statements
- If so confined, represent or could represent a substantial proportion of the financial statements
- In relation to disclosures, are fundamental to users' understanding of the financial statements

(FRC, 2025d)

Materiality: If either the omission or misstatement of an item could reasonably affect the economic decisions of users of a set of financial statements, then that item is considered material to those financial statements.

Non-sampling risk: Subtly different from sampling risk and occurs from poor interpretation of a sample by the auditor. For example, the auditor may have limited experience of sampling and may have selected a suitable sample but fails to derive the right conclusions from the data obtained (this may occur if the auditor is short of time or does not fully understand the client).

Performance materiality: The amount or amounts set by the auditor at less than materiality for the financial statements as a whole. This reduces to an appropriately low level the probability that the aggregate of uncorrected and undetected misstatements exceeds materiality for the financial statements as a whole.

Risk assessment procedures: Audit procedures designed to identify and assess the risks of material misstatement whether due to fraud or error, at both financial statement and assertion level.

Sampling risk: The risk that occurs every time a sample is selected and represents the risk that the sample does not adequately represent the population.

Chapter 4: Evidence and the audit approach

Analytical procedures: Evaluations of financial information made by a study of financial and non-financial data.

Assertions: Characteristics that all items within the financial statements (including disclosure notes) should possess in order to 'belong' there.

Audit sampling: Applying audit procedures to less than 100% of items within an account balance or class of transactions in such a way as to draw a conclusion on the account balance or class of transactions as a whole.

Audit software: Software used by the auditor to perform testing on a client's financial systems and data.

Data analytic tools: The use of technology to interrogate entire data sets.

Digital techniques in auditing: Audit techniques carried out by the auditor using a computer.

Embedded test facilities: These aim to extend the tests of control more fully throughout the period than test data and include use of a systems control and review file (SCARF) and integrated test facilities (ITF).

Integrated Test Facilities (ITF): A 'virtual' or 'dummy' copy of the system used for testing live data to confirm that it behaves in the way that it should.

Non-statistical sampling: The use of judgement to select a sample instead of a statistical technique.

Sampling units: The individual items constituting a 'population' (account balance or class of transaction) – for example, a single receivable balance within total receivables or an individual sale within total revenue.

(FRC, 2025e)

Statistical sampling: An approach to sampling that involves random selection of the sample items; and the use of probability theory to evaluate sample results including measurement of sampling risk (the risk of selecting a non-representative sample).

Stratification: Dividing a population into smaller, equal-sized sub-populations, each of which is a group of sampling units, usually by value.

Substantive testing: Audit procedures designed to detect material misstatements in the financial statements at the assertion level. They comprise of tests of detail and substantive analytical procedures.

Systems Control and Review File (SCARF): A diagnostic report of how the system is working.

Test data: The submission of 'dummy' data into the client's own system to ensure it is processed correctly, or not processed if the data is deliberately false. This can be conducted 'live' or 'dead' ie as part of normal processing or at times when the computer is not in business use.

Tests of control: Tests to obtain evidence about the effective operation of the accounting and internal control systems.

Tests of detail: Audit procedures that test classes of transaction, account balances and disclosures, usually through detailed inspection of invoices, documents and assets.

Tolerable misstatement: For **tests of control**, the tolerable misstatement is the maximum rate of deviation from a control that auditors are willing to accept in the population and still conclude that the preliminary assessment of control risk is valid. For **tests of detail** (or **substantive testing**), the tolerable misstatement is the maximum monetary error in an account balance or class of transactions that the auditor is willing to accept and still conclude that the financial statements are true and fair.

Chapter 5: Substantive testing

Accounting estimate: An approximation of the amount of an item in the absence of a precise means of measurement.

Bank reconciliation: A process designed to understand the timing differences between the entity's cash book and the bank's understanding of the entity's bank balance.

Cash and bank: Includes all bank accounts held by the entity as well as any cash amounts held on site (such as petty cash and till floats).

Circularisation: A specific technique used to test the receivables balance by writing directly to customers owing money to the audited entity and asking them to confirm what they believe they owe.

Inventory: Sub-classified as raw materials, work in progress (WIP) and finished goods.

Lease: A lease is a contract that allows an entity the right to use an asset for a period of time, in exchange for some kind of consideration.

Non-current assets: These are assets held for continuing use in the business.

Non-current liabilities: Loans repayable at a date more than one year after the year end. Examples include bank loans and debentures (generally known as borrowings).

Payables: These are amounts the company owes to its suppliers.

Trade receivables: The amount owed by customers in respect of credit sales.

Chapter 6: Reviewing and reporting findings

Deficiency in internal control: When a control is designed, implemented or operated in such a way that it is unable to prevent, or detect and correct, misstatements in the financial statements on a timely basis, or a necessary control is missing.

Bibliography

Companies Act 2006. (2006) SI 2006/46. Available from: http://www.legislation.gov.uk/ukpga/2006/46/contents [Accessed 20 February 2026].

Cressey, D.R. (1973) *Other People's Money*. New Jersey, Montclair: Patterson Smith.

Financial Conduct Authority (2019) *NatWest fined £264.8 million for anti-money laundering failures*. [Online]. Available from: https://www.fca.org.uk/news/press-releases/natwest-fined-264.8million-anti-money-laundering-failures [Accessed 20 January 2026].

Financial Reporting Council (2023) *Audit Committees and the External Audit: Minimum Standard*. [Online]. Available from: https://media.frc.org.uk/documents/Audit_Committees_and_the_External_Audit_Minimum_Standard.pdf [Accessed 20 February 2026].

Financial Reporting Council (2024) *The UK Corporate Governance Code (January 2024)* [Online]. Available from: https://media.frc.org.uk/documents/UK_Corporate_Governance_Code_2024_a2hmQmY.pdf [Accessed 20 February 2026].

Financial Reporting Council (2024a) *Glossary of terms (Auditing and Ethics) 2024*. [Online]. Available from: https://media.frc.org.uk/documents/Glossary_of_Terms_Auditing_and_Ethics_2024.pdf [Accessed 26 February 2026].

Financial Reporting Council (2025) *ISA (UK) 200 (Revised June 2016) Overall Objectives of the Independent Auditor and the Conduct of an Audit in accordance with International Standards on Auditing (UK)*. [Online]. Available from: https://media.frc.org.uk/documents/ISA_UK_200_Revised_June_2016_Updated_September_2025.pdf [Accessed 23 February 2026].

Financial Reporting Council (2025a) *ISA (UK) 240 (Revised June 2016) The Auditor's Responsibilities Relating to Fraud in an Audit of Financial Statements*. [Online]. Available from: https://media.frc.org.uk/documents/ISA_UK_240_Revised_May_2021_Updated_September_2025.pdf [Accessed 23 February 2026].

Financial Reporting Council (2025b) *ISA (UK) 315 (Revised July 2020) Identify and Assessing the Risk of Material Misstatement*. [Online]. Available from: https://media.frc.org.uk/documents/ISA_UK_315_Revised_July_2020_Updated_September_2025.pdf [Accessed 24 February 2026].

Financial Reporting Council (2025c) *ISA (UK) 320 (Revised June 2016) Materiality in Planning and Performing an Audit*. [Online]. Available from: https://media.frc.org.uk/documents/ISA_UK_320_Revised_June_2016_Updated_September_2025.pdf [Accessed 24 February 2026].

Financial Reporting Council (2025d) *ISA (UK) 705 (Revised June 2016) Modifications to the Opinion in the Independent Auditor's Report*. [Online]. Available from: https://media.frc.org.uk/documents/ISA_UK_705_Revised_June_2016_Updated_September_2025.pdf [Accessed 24 February 2026].

Financial Reporting Council (2025e) *ISA (UK) 530 Audit sampling*. [Online]. Available from: https://media.frc.org.uk/documents/ISA_UK_530_Updated_September_2025.pdf [Accessed 24 February 2026].

IAASB (2026) *About IAASB*. [Online]. Available at: https://www.iaasb.org/about-iaasb [Accessed 23 February 2026].

IFRS Foundation. (2018) *Conceptual Framework for Financial Reporting*. [Online]. Available from: https://www.ifrs.org/issued-standards/list-of-standards/conceptual-framework/#standard [Accessed 20 February 2026].

IFRS Foundation (2026) *About the International Sustainability Standards Board*. [Online]. Available at: https://www.ifrs.org/groups/international-sustainability-standards-board/ [Accessed 23 February 2026].

Proceeds of Crime Act. (2002) SI 2002/29. [Online]. Available from: http://www.legislation.gov.uk/ukpga/2002/29/contents [Accessed 20 February 2026].

Reuters (2017) *Tesco to pay £214m to settle false accounting charges.* [Online]. Available from: https://www.reuters.com/article/uk-britain-tesco-fraud-idUKKBN16Z0KD [Accessed 20 January 2026].

Rolls Royce plc (2025) *Rolls-Royce completes agreements with investigating authorities.* [Online]. Available from: https://www.rolls-royce.com/media/press-releases/2017/17-01-2017-statement.aspx [Accessed 20 January 2026].

Index

Tell us what you think

Got comments or feedback on this book? Let us know.
Use your QR code reader:

Or, visit:
https://www.smartsurvey.co.uk/s/W30E6Y/

Need to get in touch with customer service?

www.bpp.com/request-support

Spotted an error?

https://learningmedia.bpp.com/pages/errata